CIAO L'AMERICANA

A MEMOIR

ACKNOWLEDGMENTS

I wish to thank my first readers: Sally Kaplan for her brilliant and detailed insights and my long-time friend Antoinette May for her patience and wisdom which proved crucial when my enthusiasm for this whole story was waning; Monona Wali, dedicated teacher and author, who helped me mold the raw material into a story, then prodded me to stick with the story and finish it; more recently Linda Toren and Monika Rose of Manzanita Writers whose incisive comments and shared resources kept me going in the final stages. I owe the completion of this memoir to all these talented writers.

And of course, my gratitude to Carla, Franca, Vincenzo, Primo and Rita for keeping the memories alive. Enormous thanks to Maria Grazia Boldrin, who imbued every conversation with passion and humor. Her courage, artistry and humanity never failed to inspire. And always in appreciation of Morton Kaish for what he sees in everyone and everything he observes; his vision illuminates soul and body.

Italy

ISBN: 978-1-959457-19-0 (paperback)

Published in the United States by:
Blue Jay Ink, 451 A East Ojai Ave., Ojai, California 93023

CIAO L'AMERICANA
A MEMOIR

RUTH SHARI

PHONE CALL

"Don't come back to Rome now. It's not a good time."

His words, deliberate and solemn, did not sound like Ray, the man I had lived with in New York, who had followed me to Europe. It was the '70s, when we spent three weeks in Spain and three more in Italy. We became enchanted with Italy, and for different reasons, Ray and I had come to the same decision: to stay in Italy, make our lives there, and take our careers to a new level. But in this long-distance conversation, I didn't hear any enthusiasm, and certainly none of the resolve he'd shown when we admitted our mutual intentions to one another.

"It's what I want to do, too," he had made relentlessly clear. His eyes had radiated earnestness, giving me the assurance I needed that when it came to living in Italy indefinitely, we were "in it together." We were both unmoored; neither of us felt we belonged anywhere, not to any family, city or culture. We had been shedding ties to our roots, our siblings, even our mothers. More than he, I felt pressure to achieve in the conventional sense: after college, get married, launch a career, start a family, but neither of us conformed to that profile. Ray and I had each other; we were in the same adventurous mode, willing to brave the uncharted territory across the Atlantic. Yet in this moment, my arm aching from clapping the phone to my ear to hear every spoken sound, he was telling me not to come to Rome.

"What are you saying?" I asked in a wavering voice. "You know why I'm back in our old apartment. For the past month, I've done nothing but pack up and clean and get this place ready to sublet and get myself ready to move to Rome." I could feel my temperature rise, my scalp throb. My breathing stalled, waiting for his reply.

There was silence. Little messenger soldiers seemed to race back and forth between one part of my brain and the other to deliver an explanation.

"Ray, why are you telling me this?"

"It's been tough here," he said. "All our new friends have been sick. Me, too." He coughed and cleared his throat. "I'm better, getting back to normal. You wouldn't like what you see here. It's been raining for days. It's cold here in Rome."

I couldn't imagine Rome any different from the way I'd first experienced it: fountains in every piazza, the overflow trickling onto cobblestone plazas that ruined every pair of my high boots and caused me to stumble in heels. In the heat of summer, cool mists from those fountains provided relief as I walked by, watching visitors tossing coins and wading barefoot toward the larger-than-life figures that always graced water elements in Italy's cities. Rome was, to me, like an old Madame whose portly figure and wrinkled complexion never detracted from her beauty, but only drew you in more, playing on your senses. In the morning there was the reassuring smell of coffee bursting through the air, punctuating the start of day. Around lunch time, aromas of sautéing garlic and oil wafted through the alleys behind restaurant kitchens, and by nighttime, those scents mingled with women's perfumes and men's colognes as couples stepped out to dine. I reminded myself that during the three-week span of getting to know Rome and coming under its spell, it hadn't rained at all. Was Ray's news that Rome had become a cold, rainy place a bad omen? Or was he trying to tell me something?

"And there's no work, I haven't found anything. Filming seems to be on hold, at least at Cinecitta," he said.

I knew how badly Ray wanted a career in film, much more than I did. He longed to be someone other than the bartender at Joe Allen on the Upper East Side in Manhattan, serving drinks to famous actors and directors.

"Don't you think that's going to change?" I asked.

"Well, I don't know when, and meanwhile, I've run out of money," he said in a low voice. "So, you shouldn't come now, come at a better time."

I heard him take a drag on a cigarette. I lit up, too.

"Ray, you can't protect me from hard times. And it's too late not to go through with the plan. I've signed out. I have my ticket. I've said goodbye to my sister. I'm all set to leave."

"I'm warning you, baby. It's not good here."

My head began to pound, and the phone I was holding felt like a hot revolver.

"Ray, I am willing to risk it. I will find work—do anything I get hired for."

I reached for the stack of light blue Air Mail letters on my night table next to the phone cradle. When I first came back to New York for a month's stay, I received a letter from Ray every five or six days. Then there were no more letters and no calls. Was there an unwritten message I was ignoring? I wanted to let out a scream, but controlled myself; it was bad enough dealing with Ray's dismal attitude. Running up a huge tariff for this long-distance call of doom was more than I could fathom. This was the '70s, after all.

"Are you still there?" I asked softly. In the loud quiet, I could no longer hear him inhale.

"Ray, do you love me?"

Finally, he said, "Yes. But you should wait to come back to Rome."

"Ray, I'm leaving next week. Will you please be at the airport?"

"Yes, I will come for you."

"That's all I ask. We'll work through everything else. Alitalia flight #27 arriving next Thursday at 5:30 p.m."

"OK."

"See you in Rome," I said and hung up.

* * *

NEW YORK

My sister, Marie, looked at me without expression, stiffening up when I confessed to her that except for the clothes I was taking, nothing in the studio apartment meant anything to me, and leaving it behind gave me a sense of starting over. I could read her thoughts: *It's so easy for you to cut the ties; you leave with no other baggage than your suitcases.* Maybe she felt I was being irresponsible, saddling her with the job of finding a proper tenant, collecting the rent, and handling any problems from the sublet of my studio apartment. I hugged her, seeing how protective she was, how grateful I needed to be. We went down the elevator to the street where she hailed a taxi to go back to her place in the upper East 70s.

The sun was just slipping below the horizon to mark the subdued pace of Saturday night in Manhattan; with so many people out of town, it was calm compared to week nights. When we lived together in Manhattan, Ray and I had a treasured ritual. With him at work from 4 o'clock on, I'd prowl about our small flat, hanging up his jacket and brushing my suede boots. I put away dishes, scrubbed the tile of the bathroom floor on my hands and knees, trekked to the basement to use the coin operated laundry machines and then took a shower and washed my hair—all to kill time until my evening with Ray could begin. Ray would call me right before he left the restaurant, glasses at the bar washed and shined and stored, liquor bottles wiped down, stainless sink drained and polished, the customers and wait staff gone. As the last one to leave, he had to close up:

"Hey hon, I am leaving shortly, should be there by quarter to one, latest."

"Ok, I'll grab a booth."

I would taxi across town, and Ray would find me sitting in the darkness of The Flick, looking at the neon displays and game machines. It was the only place of its kind in Manhattan: Open from 5 p.m. to 2 a.m., The Flick was one quarter casino, two quarters ice cream parlor, and a mysterious upstairs where we had never ventured except to visit the restrooms.

In spite of the hour, Ray never seemed tired. He'd slide into the booth across from me and give me a penetrating gaze, his eyes reflecting the light from the glass fixture hanging over the center of the table. He'd take my hands and cup them in his.

"What have you been up to?" he often said. It would not have mattered what I had done before meeting him at an hour when most people were in bed. Ray trusted me and he appreciated my trust in him. I could read it on his face. He made me feel comfortable.

"Nothing much," I usually reported, squeezing his fingers. "There's always a lot to do around the apartment. I couldn't wait for you to get off work tonight. To tell you the truth, sometimes I find it hard keeping busy till midnight."

"Well, it won't always be like this, my tending bar and you having to wait till midnight to go out on a date. Things are gonna change, I know they will." His voice took on a huskier tone when he spoke about a future different from the present, as if he were commanding his fate to change so that he could begin to live the life he dreamed of. Director, producer, deal maker, it was always something grand with Ray. And I believe he wanted to reassure me that his being broke and my being broke—I was an aspiring actor doing more auditions than actual stage work—were temporary circumstances.

Ray and I didn't have to look at the menu. We knew it by heart and always had the same thing. When the waitress came over wearing a mini skirt, skinny top and high heels, we ordered the ice cream dish we each wanted. Mine was Number 25, his Number 26. Both were on The Flick's menu of Sundae boats, consisting of four scoops of ice-cream, a mixture of coffee and vanilla flavors, mine topped with butterscotch, his with hot fudge, plus pecans and walnuts.

We would devour our 5000-calorie experience in silence, savoring the cold ice cream on our tongues and ladling the hot butterscotch and chocolate sauce on the crown of each scoop to soften it. We were happy being there, eating ice cream at 1:30 in the morning. We had no rules about the right sort of date. In those days, we didn't care about eating the right thing, either; we were young, healthy and strong, and did as we pleased. The only wistfulness was hinted at by Ray, who wanted to be able to take me out on Saturday night instead of tending bar. But I was satisfied with our odd ritual, earnest play mixed with daring; it was an invention of our very own. I was 26, and Ray was my first real boyfriend---the first guy I'd ever lived with, and he treated me as an equal. We were chums. Living with him in New York City especially in the '70s, quieted my fears of the big city and made me feel more secure.

Ray had Sundays off, and we'd sleep until about noon, then I'd make coffee and pancakes and we'd read the *New York Times*. By 7 p.m., dressed to the nines, we'd go out to a dance club. Ray had trained in the studios of Arthur Murray in Lake Placid where he grew up, a relatively small town where ballroom dancing was a major pastime. One of his many odd jobs over the years had been as a dance instructor. So he knew how to dance. I didn't. I had good rhythm, and when we were on the dance floor, Ray led so clearly and expertly that I was able to follow him. The nightclub where we danced every Sunday had no cover charge, which allowed us to order ginger ale and club soda and keep dancing all night until we were completely exhausted, often until 11 or 12. Dancing with Ray wasn't a smoochy, body glove romantic experience; it was an execution of choreography. I needed to follow the steps and turns he led. While he had me in his arms, he was in control. He commanded me. Every new song and rhythm pattern involved his direction. He would have me repeat what he taught until my feet moved in sync with his. Many times, Ray and I became the center of attention, putting on a show, thanks to his spins and dips. The other dancers would give us space by clearing to the edge of the dance floor where they'd stand and watch us move. Ray made me shine.

***

Ciao L'Americana

ROME

R ay met me at Fiumicino International Airport in Rome. He looked like a different man. He was wearing a new brown leather jacket and brown pants. His curly auburn hair was overgrown, much longer than usual, his too white skin was dotted with more dark freckles than I'd ever noticed, yet overall, he had taken on some of the sheen of the classy Italian male. He gave me a hug, not a kiss. His eyes, normally brimming with warmth, avoided mine. When I threw my arms around him, he didn't soften at all, but stood straight, and then held me away from him with rigid arms. As he looked into my face, I couldn't tell if he perceived my sense of relief mixed with excitement despite the fact that I was trying hard not to show emotion. We stood facing each other, closer now, and he moved my hair behind each one of my ears, not saying anything. His mouth and the set of his jaw seemed to relax for only an instant. Then he turned toward the black slide just beginning to plop a plane load of luggage onto the carousel.

I pointed out my four large suitcases as they clambered down to the outer ring and then tried to help him load two luggage carts. He insisted on doing it himself; he was strong. I grabbed the smallest valise and my make up case and set them on top of one of the carts so that I could easily push it along as we headed to the taxi queue. Ray gave the driver a street address in his laughable Italian—he was still trying to impress me. The driver nodded in acknowledgment and off we sped at around 6 p.m. on that overcast November day. Ray sat by the door, a wide distance from me. I collapsed in the opposite corner, rumpled and drained, partly from the long flight and partly from the letdown. Ray started to talk. He told me he'd found a place for us to live, beyond Trastevere in the near outskirts of the city. I was glad he had arranged our living situation, even if it meant living far from the heart of Rome and having to take a bus or a taxi to get into the city center. If I were less exhausted, I would let go of my attachment to how sweet it had been living in central Rome in the small Hotel Portoghese only two months ago. It was the least expensive hotel we could find; a tad seedy, but clean enough. Every day, I used to shop for fresh bread, yogurt, fresh fruit, cheese, cold meats and other salumerie, which would be our breakfast and lunch. That was the way we saved money. And then we ate dinner in a small trattoria off the Piazza Navona, not far from the hotel. It wasn't fancy, but we found the food in Rome was always delicious in any eatery anywhere, it didn't matter how simple.

"So, our landlady is Olga, an older woman and very kind, at least that's how I see her," he said. "She's old fashioned, maybe a little strict for you. So, you're going to have to act like a Signora." he said between puffs of a cigarette.

"Oh my God, Ray. What do you mean, act like the Signora?" He made a face and wrinkled his nose, gazing out the window.

"Isn't it insane that in Italy in this day and age, any couple who sleep in the same bedroom are expected to be married?" I said.

Ray didn't appear to share my astonishment. I could feel him bristling. He darted his eyes at me, then said: "I really think we should pretend that it's true or Olga will be offended. I don't want to offend her."

It occurred to me that in conversation with Olga, Ray must have referred to me as *the signora*. His unexpected advice and concern about our unmarried status was beginning to make sense.

"Just to make sure she's okay with the situation, I paid her two months' rent up front," he said.

No wonder he's uptight, I thought. *He's broke.* I murmured in sympathy and reached for his hand, covering it firmly with my own.

"Once we drop off the luggage and freshen up, why don't we go out to dinner? My treat," I offered.

By the time we arrived, it was dark. All I could see was a building whose façade had hints of a finer past when it may have been someone's grand residence. The dim light at the entrance cast an eerie spell on its rickety stone steps. Ray led me to a small wing on the left, our flat, which shared an entrance with another little apartment. We cleaned up quickly. Cold water on my face, fresh make up, clean teeth and a silk scarf pulled from my handbag recharged my energy. I was famished after more than 24 hours without a good meal.

We headed out again, taking another taxi, and I pressed money into Ray's hands for the fare. He told the driver to take us to the same restaurant in the Piazza Navona where we'd always dined. We were the first ones to be seated, at around 7:45, early for dinner in Rome. The waiter brought warm crusty bread, *acqua minerale* and the menu. Ray and I stared at the menu. After a minute, Ray put his aside and commented that he hadn't been there since the last time with me. While I made my menu choices, he lit a Gitane, and before it was finished, he stubbed it out and lit another.

"*Vino bianco o rosso,*" the waiter asked.

"Bee an ko. Mezo," Ray said, indicating a half carafe with his hands. A moment later, the waiter came back, poured us white wine, and I was gulping it. I raised my glass to Ray's and we touched glasses without making a toast. Ray was looking nervous and uncomfortable, his hands fidgeting with the soft blue pack of Gitanes. When the waiter returned, Ray asked him what his name was.

"*Giovanni. Piacere mio,*" the waiter said politely. "*Cosa si prende?*"

(What will you have?) We ordered, and I looked around the restaurant, a familiar place that could offer me a sense of comfort and sameness. A group of four entered and sat at the other end of the room.

"Where's Pasquale?" I whispered to Ray. He shook his head. Our favorite waiter had always worked the evening meal; the only day he didn't work was when the restaurant took its mandatory day off, according to labor regulations in Italy. Could Pasquale have quit, gone somewhere else? He always treated us like his favorite foreign couple, anticipating our need for more mineral water, another carafe of house wine, wanting to know why we hadn't finished every bit of food on our plates, a rare occurrence. Tonight, I would miss the sampler of cakes and dessert concoctions—not pristine or large enough to be a normal portion—that Pasquale would present just to us at the end of every dinner. He had figured out that Ray and I had a strong sweet tooth but weak pockets. Without any formal airs, only a small flourish, he would set down the dessert plate, saying: "*Eccolo*," placing two forks side by side on the table. I missed how he took care of us. Maybe Ray was right when he said things in Rome had changed.

***

Ciao L'Americana

CONFESSION

"Hon, there is something I have to tell you," Ray said, looking down at the tablecloth, his hands lighting up a new Gitane before stubbing out the old one. "I met someone while you were gone."

"How did you meet her?" I said as evenly as I could.

He lifted his head and faced me, but he looked as though he were bracing himself for a blow, pushing his chair back a few inches, his eyes skimming the door for a second and then coming back to me.

"She was here on business with her father, who is head of a big corporation. She was charming, very energetic and full of confidence about the future. Seemed like she had her act together," Ray said.

"And so, what does that have to do with *us*?" I blurted out before I realized how stupid the question was.

"It has a lot to do with us," he said, clasping his square, sturdy hands together, for a moment not fingering a cigarette.

I gasped out loud and then let out a huge breath. Was I really hearing this?

Ray was a sweet guy, and we had made a pact to try this new life in Rome together. I dubbed him a "regular" guy, the term I used for a man who treated me with love and respect. I felt we were equals. And it wasn't all about sex with him; we were each other's best friend, certainly for me the first such experience with a man. My regular guy called his mother regularly, too, and when I overheard their conversation, he acted very protective, a good sign I thought. I found Ray was "into" me; when we were out, he appeared to only have eyes for me. I never worried about losing him. Had I taken him for granted? Had I lost my allure, taken up as I was with my own struggle to succeed in New York: going on auditions, trying out for everything, even "extra" work, pounding the pavement to get modeling work? In starting over in Rome, I had courage, yes, but not full confidence in the future. So, I was different from the woman Ray was describing.

"Is that why you didn't want me to come to Rome?" I said with an edge of *ah, ha.* I detested the thought that Ray had tried to sabotage my return to Rome because he planned to ditch me for some new chick. "How did it happen? I mean, what happened?" I asked.

"Well, after you left, autumn rolled into Rome, and the tourists went away. Like I said, it was dreary, cold and rainy. I had nothing going on. I was running out of options for work and running out of money. And you were gone. Here was this American who came on strong with me, smacking of wealth, staying in expensive hotels, accompanying her father on business, surrounded by rich people and introducing me to a few of them. She just seemed to spill over with success," he said.

"Oh, Ray," was all I could say, realizing that any more from him and I would plunge to a deep low point from the merciful high I'd been riding from the moment I'd boarded the plane to Rome.

"I am not proud of what happened, but I had to tell you," he said, downing the remaining wine in his glass and pouring another for both of us.

The waiter came by with the food and I begged him to serve it in a few minutes, explaining in Italian that we were dealing with a crisis, *una gran tragedia* were the words I used, hoping he'd think we'd had a death in the family. For what seemed like ten minutes, neither of us said a word.

"I went to bed with her," he said, catching my eyes, then turning away.

"Where is she now? "I asked, keeping my eyes on his averted face, wishing my gaze could dispel his immutable admission. I suddenly felt a burning sensation in my cheeks. I put the outside of my palm against one throbbing cheek and closed my eyes for a few seconds. "Will you still be seeing her?"

"No, she's back in the States. It's over," he said, searching my eyes. "I'm sorry I had to tell you this. But it was important to clear the air."

I pulled all the way back into my seat, moving my legs under the table until I could no longer feel my thighs touching his. The more I fought to keep control, the more tears came. From the corner of my blurred vision, I saw the waiter coming toward us, and then quickly walking away. Ray was lighting two Gitanes and handing me one. I shook my head. I wanted a filter cigarette, not a Gitane.

"Hon, it's over with that girl," he said, still holding out a cigarette. "I **will** make it up to you."

I wanted to believe him. Ray was my anchor. But could I trust him? Was he still mine?.

***

PIAZZA NAVONA

I paid the bill and we left the restaurant, our waiter ushering us out saying, "*Buona Notte*" and holding the door open for me as I walked out ahead of Ray. I heard a tinge of sympathy in his voice, and he seemed to perceive something beneath my pretext of "*gran tragedia.*" He had likely studied my face, and mine was one that readily revealed my emotions: I was easy to read. My first acting teacher in New York had always harped on me for conveying too much expression. She often sternly warned that I needed to emote with restraint.

"For you to show the character's feelings, you have also to be genuine," she declared in her thick Russian accent. "You are a terrible pretender," were her exact words. So, it hadn't been difficult for Giovanni, hovering around our table tonight, to sense that I was wounded. In the months I'd lived in Rome; I'd noticed a distinctive trait in the Italians—their sensitivity to human emotion. Even as he waited on us for the first time, Giovanni had shown kindness, empathy and good timing that was well beyond the average stranger's capacity.

Once on the street, Ray and I started moving instinctively toward the Piazza Navona. We'd always known the piazza to have a piercing vitality. Could walking in that lively piazza—always an experience so *simpatica*—console me now? In the Piazza Navona, a person could find anyone from anywhere: Romans of every class, as well as tourists and expatriates from England, Germany or the U.S. The piazza housed ancient, stately buildings facing the square whose ground floor arcades were set up as sidewalk cafés. Open from 11 a.m. to 12 midnight, they served espresso, cappuccino and morning brioches, in the afternoon *amaro* or *aperitivo di moda*, which drink seemed to change every season, plus eighteen flavors of gelato and pastries all day long.

Our tentative pace matched those who were out for a stroll, *una passeggiata*. People in Rome moved slowly, as though they had no momentum to get from one place to the next. They walked easily and without haste; whereas for me, it was an effort to move at all. I felt as though I were floating, not really putting feet on the ground. When I looked down and around me, I was surprised to find myself still standing with Ray next to me. We circled the piazza and when I paused, I must have appeared ready to keel over, for Ray took my arm and led us to a taxi stand. His pale face had some color now, as if finally good blood had started to course through his veins. I saw that he was walking with his usual gracefulness, his arms swinging naturally. Perhaps a great weight had been lifted from him. It had shifted onto me, it seemed. I wondered if he could sense my disorientation. I felt my internal compass had been swallowed by the sea, leaving me to hold my balance in rough waters that flowed toward a rocky shore.

"It's 10 o'clock Roman time," Ray said gently.

Adjusted for New York time, it was a whole day earlier. I'd been up for two days.

Inside the cab, I couldn't think of anything to say, even if the silence was killing me. Why did I have to learn about his infidelity on the first night back in Rome? It had been reassuring—even if I barely admitted it to myself—that I would cobble together a new future in a foreign land with someone I loved. No longer could I feel reassured. Sitting in the taxi was torture because it required me to be still, as though nothing had happened. Instead, I wanted to shout and scream and pound the window. I had an urge to stand up while the taxi was moving, in protest of these cursed new circumstances, the indignity of Ray's betrayal.

Back in the new apartment, I opened a suitcase and delved for a nightgown, not realizing I'd placed it on top along with a bathrobe. I don't remember how I again found the bathroom, where I sloppily brushed my teeth and folded my hair up with a barrette, too tired to clean my face. The bathroom tile felt cold to my bare feet and the incandescent light over the mirror was dim—the better not to look into the mirror. My skin was drained of all its color and looked bluish. I groaned.

"If you want, I'll sleep on the couch," Ray said. He was still dressed, his dark trousers and leather jacket as pristine as when I first saw him at the airport.

"The couch looks too short for you. And it's cold in the big room: It's cold everywhere," I said, wrapping my arms around me. I eyed the European sized double bed, small by U.S. standards; it looked too short for our long-legged bodies.

"But it's up to you. I'm so tired, I really don't care," I said.

He took the final two drags of his cigarette at once, stubbed it out, went into the bathroom and then came to bed, wearing his white jockey shorts. Ray never slept in pajamas. We both just lay there on our backs, not touching, facing the ceiling in the dark, covers pulled up to keep me from trembling in the cold. Now and then a cat howled outside the building. Then a trio of cats would snarl back. Then silence, followed by massive hissing and a litany of wailing. I couldn't turn my mind off and, turbulent as I was, I couldn't fall asleep. The unfamiliar sounds of cats stalking in the night was unnerving to me. As my eyes traced the flashes of moonlight streaming through the blinds, I considered a plan to move out the next day. But where would I go? *Think about it*, a voice in my head said. From the phone call in New York that now seemed so long ago, which had been pregnant with meaning, I had claimed

Ciao L'Americana

my resolve to be in Rome. I recognized that neither wild stallions nor lions roaring in the catacombs of the Coliseum could have kept me from returning to Rome. *Be practical*, another inner voice chimed in. Was I brave enough to move forward by myself? *Damn him, damn the man*, I cursed to myself. My chest rose and emptied with a heavy sigh. There was venom in my throat that I wanted to spit at Ray as I silently wished him a sleepless night.

"Hon, what's wrong?" Ray finally said from his side of the bed, his head still facing the ceiling.

"I'm tired, I am shocked," I said. "How did you think I would feel? Is this any way to come back to begin our life together in Rome?" I turned away to lie on my side, fighting back tears, burning tears that might have ushered in the answers to my questions with searing truthfulness. Bad as his news had been, while I lay there in the same bed with Ray as I had for the past two years, I didn't want to leave, not without knowing where to go. But mostly, I didn't want to go it alone, which seemed like double punishment: the first from his unfaithfulness, the second because I would be surrendering my dream to live in Rome.

I felt Ray reach around for my hand and clasp it tightly. His fingers were warm and enveloping as he placed our two hands against his shoulder and snuggled his chest against my back. I didn't resist. He had said he would make it up to me, he did say he would make it up to me, I muttered soundlessly to myself. Until I fell asleep.

***

FIRST MORNING

When I woke up the next morning, Ray was gone. I felt dread pour into me. Was he kind or cruel to have let me sleep in and wake up alone in unfamiliar surroundings? I looked for a clock and found none. The flat Ray had chosen for us was shabbier by morning than at night, and it was dark and gloomy. My trusty Bulova watch lying on top of my sweater was the brightest spot within reach. I grabbed the watch: 10 a.m. My clothes were draped over a faded upholstered chair, threads protruding from a lumpy seat, its carved wood frame scratched on all sides. Suddenly I felt hungry—neither of us had really eaten last night—and needed the bathroom, which I could not see. Ray's leather jacket was gone. *He left me on the first morning we could have woken up together after nearly two months of being apart.* There was a note taped to the inside of the front door: **Bathroom down the hall on the left. Don't forget to be extra nice to landlady Olga.**

How annoying of Ray to want to placate the landlady when he should be placating me. In that moment, I had no concept of how difficult it'd been for Ray to find this flat. He was a foreigner with no job, no bank account or credit history and likely no local reference or co-sponsor. How had he managed? I remember from my first meeting Ray in New York City that he lived a gypsy lifestyle. He seemed unencumbered, a free spirit, excited about our connecting, and ready to ignite our relationship. I was immediately taken. His eyes were golden and his gaze reached inside me and drew me in. He could ease my anxiousness with one long look. When he'd moved in with me, he carried all his possessions in just two suitcases. I suspected he had never had his own place, whereas I had been living on my own for years. Yet the City frightened me, especially when I had to take the subway, which filled me with terror. I hated the roar of the underground trains, the foul smells of urine and vomit vaping off the filthy interior concrete stairs. New York's unrelenting noise, itself a defining feature of urban life, was unsettling: sirens going off every ten minutes, the mad pace of the average pedestrian and the recklessness of speeding cab drivers. Living with Ray in my tiny flat at 71st Street and West End Avenue—the best location I could afford as an aspiring actor—I had begun to relax more often. Ray gave me a sense of being looked after; although I still maintained a constant vigilance as I hurried about the streets of New York.

The nagging feeling of peril now—partly due to unfamiliar turf, partly from the fear of abandonment—was aroused in me that first morning in Rome after my return. What if Ray had left me? Suddenly I was wide awake, tightening my robe around me for warmth and swallowing the lump in my throat as I considered my options, feeling alone, desolate. Staying with a girlfriend in Rome was out of the question for I hadn't yet made any close women friends, and if I had, they'd still be living with their parents if they were single. Going back home was the least possible course of action. It would have been an admission of defeat in giving up on my deep desire to live in Italy. Then, too, I no longer had a home in New York, for my studio had been subleased.

I resisted my inclination to call my sister to seek her advice. I knew she was secretly fearful that I would do something rash, like marry Ray. To her, he was just a talker with big dreams, which didn't impress her as long as he was the bartender at Joe Allen's. I suspected she considered him a shiftless mooch with nothing to offer her baby sister. Whenever I saw my sister, we avoided the topic of "the future," for I knew I couldn't give her the answers she wanted to hear. As much as she was my strongest advocate, I felt too much mothering and too little encouragement from Marie. I needed to spread my wings, and finally, at age 26, I had a live-in boyfriend. He didn't have money or a university degree. But whatever he had, he shared, bringing home gourmet food from the restaurant, paying for cabs when we went out at night and finding unique, affordable ways for us to have a good time. We had fun together, delighting in our private rituals, ways of playing that were small but satisfying celebrations. Would it work the same way in Rome?

Just then, Ray walked in, carrying a bag of warm brioches that he waved in front of my nose. "Ahhhh, mmm," I salivated, opening the bag and grabbing one, tearing it apart. I looked at Ray, who was fingering clothes in a drawer, and before I could ask him where the coffee was, Ray was organizing the day:

"Get dressed, hon. You can shower first because we need to get going. We'll have coffee and lunch at the restaurant. I want you to meet my new friends at the Trattoria del Corso."

An hour later, we took a taxi into the center, and it was an alarmingly long ride. I hated to think it meant the flat was in an isolated location far from everything. I was used to the compressed living conditions of New York City where everything was within close reach.

The trattoria was off the Via del Corso. It was a mélange of family eatery and American diner with pale plastic table tops, vinyl flooring and bright overhead lights. From its street corner location, noisy vehicles were always in full view through large glass panels. Ray had connected with a small group of local people who gathered at meal times; it had obviously become his hangout. The owner, Armando, was a soft-spoken man of few words, more mild mannered, I noticed, than many native Romans. Always dressed in a brown or dark grey jacket, there seemed not to be one bone in his short stocky body that exhibited the exaggerated behavior and overstated promises Ray and I had observed among typical Roman men. Most appeared eager to play the grand host in our presence or maybe even impress us, the new foreigners. This behavior is called *"fare bella figura,"* to come out looking good, a strong Italian trait. Armando spoke no English, but he was receptive to my modest use of the Italian language and quick to indicate that he understood.

Ray and I continued to go to the trattoria and took all our meals there, at whose expense I never learned until much later, after weeks had passed. I knew that we needed this haven, a place indoors to rest and be restored. Rome had changed, as though a pale grey shadow had descended. There were fewer colors to imbibe, no tourists floundering around shouting and even the fountains flowed less robustly. It was November now, and in the autumn months it rains in sunny Rome, and much to my chagrin, it is cold.

American Thanksgiving was nearing, and for the first time for each of us, it would be spent far away from home. I kept a close eye on Ray, who was hard to read when he was in a "down mood." I tried to detect his state of mind from the way he quelled his anxiety with boisterous joking around to coax others to laugh.

I can still visualize him sitting at a mottled Formica table, wearing a chocolate brown turtleneck sweater, his auburn hair longer and curlier than ever as he pushed it off his cheeks and pressed his white knuckles against his freckled skin. He would focus intently on anyone seated in front of him, jabbering away at them to induce a smile or a laugh. When he achieved that response, it meant he'd made a new friend. Somehow, he succeeded in winning people over even without speaking Italian, except for a few pat phrases like: *Piacere.* Or *Mi piace* or *Ci vediamo* or *Mille grazie.* Men, in particular, engaged with Ray.

The trattoria became the place where Ray was finding a small audience; it was very much his scene, although we went there together every night without fail. Otherwise, we wouldn't have eaten. I went along with Ray's arrangements, and my presence as his girlfriend was well accepted. To the Italians, Ray presented me as his *fidanzata* (fiancée) because there is no word in Italian for girlfriend. Unknowingly, I had gained a new respect.

∗∗∗

POSITANO

Tensions between us gradually eased as Ray and I shared a flat and the same unspoken anxieties: how would we find work, how long would the money last, how far could we go with the little we had? Neither of us mentioned these worries to our new friends. I was less guarded than Ray, but, like him, kept up the appearance of well-being, truly uneasy about admitting to friends and acquaintances that we lived "hand to mouth." Ray continued with his antics, but I could sense that the more he joked around, the more anxious he was. Our Italian friends were mercifully polite, never directly asking us about work or what we were cobbling together. I had fast dwindling savings supplemented every couple of months by a small check from my sister covering the difference between the rent collected subletting my flat in New York and the rent I actually paid. As for the apartment on the outskirts of Rome that I dreaded living in, Ray had pre-paid the rent. I pondered how he could have managed it without any savings. Somehow, he was paying for our meals at the Trattoria, too, for we were never presented with a bill. I attributed his assuming these financial responsibilities to his promise "to make it up to me" for his cheating heart when I was away in New York.

I felt I needed to do my part to support us. *Now it's my turn.* I decided to look for work, to put myself *out there* as we used to say in the acting community and in the world of modeling. The two went together; modeling had proved a lucrative way for me to make money in New York while waiting for the "big break" in theater.

I started making the rounds of modeling agencies, carrying my heavy brown leather model's portfolio, introducing myself and leaving behind my one-page, two-sided photo composite sheet that presented black and white images of me in a variety of settings, wearing fashions that illustrated different moods and activities. Interviewing was not just showing up physically, but also a call to dazzle those who booked talent. I needed a certain degree of charm, energy and humility to persuade the agency to find me work. The rest was a waiting game. Calling on the agencies motivated me. I believed I would be hired; after all, I'd worked in the most professional of all markets. I reached out as well to everyone in our little group who knew anybody who knew anyone in fashion, film or theater. I assaulted new people, too, whose curiosity upon first meeting me, the enduring visitor, usually spurred me to explain that I was a working model just in from New York to begin modeling in Rome. That often prompted a series of good wishes and compliments. Within a couple of weeks, I landed a job offer. The agency said it involved going on location to Positano, a few hours south of Rome outside of Naples right on the Terranean Sea. A new designer had just created a fashion line and was set to introduce it in a dramatized format. The only hitch was that it didn't pay. All expenses to and from the Amalfi Coast would be compensated, such as train transportation, hotel and meals. But no salary. There would be two days of rehearsal and four shows over a long weekend for a total of six days on location in Positano. How could I consider working for nothing when I had made a mint as a model in New York? I struggled to figure out what mattered more to me: was it the experience of my first job in Italy—on the Amalfi Coast no less—which filled me with a level of excitement long unaroused, or was it being paid for the job? I had found this first job easily enough and had faith it would lead quickly to more work and better jobs.

Feeling jazzed and ready to strut my stuff in Italy, off I went to Positano, kissing Ray goodbye and promising to call every day, even as I sensed he was wishing that he'd been chosen to work on location.

***

The clothing designer had a theater director's approach to showing off clothes. He put his models on stage in what had become a defunct theater situated in the bowels of *Napoli*. He encouraged us to move the way we felt naturally in response to his music selections—jazz and rhythm 'n' blues, which were played loudly. He had me wear a curly red-haired wig and many short-skirted outfits with knee high leather boots. His clothes took on a distinctive flare depending on the model. It was the antithesis of the stereotypic elevated runway show featuring dead faced models slinking their skinny bodies along the platform. When I was on stage, I felt comfortable, sporting my new identity with the wild red wig. I could play the comedienne, improvising and using a strong sense of timing that came effortlessly, surprising even me. I was learning about my stage presence.

Of course, I wanted to share that with Ray. I called him from the pay phone booth, urging him to join me.

"Hey, baby, come see it. It's more like a comedy sketch than runway modeling—you'll love it. Besides, Ray, Positano is beautiful, a jewel perched on the side of the steep rocky coast. Every little house seems nestled into the mountain and the view changes every hour. It's different every time you look at the coastline. I've never seen any place like it."

"I can't, hon. I need to be in Rome in case anything comes up for me." I called the next day and the next, always hearing that he couldn't leave Rome. Finally, he agreed.

"OK. I'll be down Saturday, but I have to come right back on

Sunday night."

My final show was Sunday night, and his truncated visit meant that he wouldn't be sharing the excitement at the end of the run. We wouldn't be traveling together back to Rome, which to me was a wasted opportunity. Still, I consoled myself that at least he'd be joining me in Positano and seeing me in the show.

Ray may have been duly struck by my funny bits on stage for which I sensed the audience leaning in, those improvised bits creating a hush. I noticed him staring at me, his eyes bulging. My comic flourishes marked the scene and I had set myself apart. Since Ray had never seen me perform in anything, I was eager to hear his reaction. He must have noticed how much fun I was having onstage, yet he remained strangely silent. Unable to bear his restraint, I shrieked: "What d'ya think?"

"You did good, hon," he said quietly. "They should be paying you."

This felt like a thwarted compliment, tinged with jealousy. No matter, I refused to let him deflate my spirit; it was my gig and I had done it well.

***

Ciao L'Americana

TRATTORIA DEL CORSO

A mong the friends Ray had made was Umberto, a painter. He was a little shorter than I was, around 5'6" and had big brown eyes and long wavy brown hair with a bang that covered his forehead except when he swept it back with his fingers, which was often. Umberto, who was about our age, was the reserved, brooding artist type, intense when he finally spoke. I felt he was devouring me with his eyes, sizing me up with a penetrating gaze. Before we'd exchanged words, he had assessed my face.

"Your mouth isn't even, the left lip is lower than the right," he said, as though I were some subject in a life drawing class he needed to study and sketch. His raw frankness was unsettling and drew out every ounce of my insecurity. In response, I took my mirror and saw that in outlining my lips with a pencil, I hadn't drawn each side the same. It must have been the dim light in that old hall bathroom at the flat, I thought. I couldn't take Umberto's scrutiny; I began to keep my distance from him. Ray, on the other hand, was rhapsodic about knowing a painter and having him at our table. I doubted if he'd ever known a painter who worked on canvas instead of house walls. Ray treated Umberto with exaggerated respect, pulling out his chair and ordering the wine as soon as 'Berto showed up.

Seeing me with Ray at my side must have conveyed to 'Berto that we were a couple, that I had a place in Ray's world. He eventually backed off from staring at me and criticizing my appearance. Despite a distinctive style that included wearing jumpsuits, knee high leather boots, wide brimmed hats and the occasional mini skirt, my appearance was now accepted by 'Berto without comment. In fact, I learned he knew a journalist who wrote for the entertainment section of one of Rome's daily newspapers. He gushed about how a little favorable publicity could help launch my career. I hoped it wasn't empty promises.

Soon after the special modeling assignment in Positano, the tone of my visits to the Trattoria changed. I was met with exuberance: "*Eccola:*" Here she comes! There was an unspoken "Wow" which our gang emoted with flourishes that sounded like gurgles and trills. Umberto rose to give me a hug and I wondered what had come over our sometimes morose painter friend, who had never hugged me before. I was grateful for his warmth and hugged him back. He beamed at me. Did he have good news? He said that his journalist buddy Gaetano wanted to meet very soon to do a story on me that would generate publicity. My second break might be taking place just in the nick of time! I rejoiced within my own heart. I wasn't certain what "very soon" meant—would it be this year or next? This was Rome, after all. There was a different concept of time in the land of *Domani*. Christmas was coming—my first spent abroad—and I felt oddly out of sorts.

***

Instead of being thrilled to spend my first Christmas in Rome, I felt detached, no enthusiasm bubbled up. Christmas **a Roma** didn't have that zing. Streets and storefronts were not decorated. Only a handful of shops, like those on the Via dei Condotti which catered to foreigners from the U.S., placed shiny glass balls in the window and decked the front door with a large velvet bow. There were no trees or wreaths, no strung lights. Without the buzz of the U.S. style "***holidaze***" I couldn't pick up the spirit of the season; i.e., the gift giving season. Without money, how would I come up with gifts, even small ones, to give to our landlady Olga, the few friends who'd taken us out and showed kindness, and the regulars at dinner like Umberto and the trattoria's owner, Armando? I withdrew into myself, musing: hadn't I moved to Italy to experience something different?

Sensing my heavy spirit, Ray decided around the middle of December that it was too close to the holidays to "sweat" his not getting calls or interviews for work. He announced that the following Saturday he'd made plans for us to step out on the town. He was arranging for us to go to the Osteria del Orso, a swank place you couldn't get into unless you knew someone, according to Ray.

"Who do you know of that caliber?" I asked, no longer as suscep-tible to the broad strokes inherent in Ray's overstatements; I knew he could fabricate. However, he was right that everything was more or less "on hold." I was still waiting for Umberto to connect me with his journalist friend. The tourists were long gone. Life had returned to its normal slow moving Roman pace.

"Armando made us reservations at Osteria del Orso. He's got lots of contacts in the restaurant world. He knows the Maitre d' who works there. The place has music and dancing, hon. And it's dressy."

It was the best proposal Ray had made in a long time—he knew how to get to me—just as my patience was running out and my imag-ination was stalling. We owed ourselves a night on the town.

***

OSTERIA DEL ORSO

That December night we got dressed up for the first time since arriving in Italy in September, which now seemed long ago. I put on a pale fuchsia, silk satin dress with a wide belt that cinched my waist. It had a fluted collar, deep V neck and long cuffed sleeves. Ray, ever in his turtleneck knits and black denim pants, finally put on a dress shirt, a pair of gabardine slacks I'd never seen before, and donned a navy-blue blazer, virtually the closest thing to a suit he could put together. We took a cab to Osteria del Orso, another long ride into the heart of Rome and were dropped off at a *vicolo* that was closed to traffic. It was literally a street so tiny it was like a paved corridor that led nowhere. The entrance was still and eerily silent: Could it be an unpublished address? The front door was easy to miss and the name of the restaurant and night club appeared faintly on a burnished bronze plaque attached to the stone façade. To say the interior was swank was understating it. There were beige velour and leather banquettes, crystal chandeliers above the middle of the main salon and sculpted gilt sconces which you could imagine once held candles but were now incandescent lighting. The walls and furnishings were of a monochromatic color scheme that created a sense of warmth and welcome as well as anticipated intimacy. My eyes had been transfixed by the dignified busts perched on marble shelves and the duly worn velvet couches in the foyer which suggested a former use as someone's private mansion. I surveyed the dining room, quite large, but broken at angles to create private spaces, and when I saw the polished wood dance floor, I grabbed Ray's hand and squeezed it. He smiled with his lips closed and took my arm as we followed the maitre d' to our table. Ray looked proud, proud that he could finally offer me what he felt I deserved.

It was still mildly strained between us—the sting of Ray's betrayal was like a faded but ever-present scar. I still struggled to shake off the hesitancy I sometimes had about launching into my new life in Rome while often feeling uncertainty about the man with whom I'd expected to make that life. In my most headstrong moment, I was prone to believing there was no turning back, only going forward. I had continued to busy myself with learning to get around alone by bus. It was always a challenge to remain unbothered by the local Romans, some of whom stared at me, others who hooted from inside their cars and still others, who passing me on the sidewalk, turned back to look and would make comments amongst themselves. I was quick to pick up more of the Italian language. I fell in as much as possible by day with Ray's routine, his friends, his forum at the Trattoria. By night, we were usually spent. The rental flat always depressed me. Sometimes we made love, and it seemed genuine on his part. On my side, I held back, still fearing he might not love me to the core. What proof did I have from Ray? He said things to make me laugh, rather than seduce me with tender words, which I might have construed as the words of a smitten man. It continued to cross my mind that if he found a gigantic opportunity to get where he thought he wanted to be, Ray would not hesitate to take it, even if it meant sleeping with some new girl before ditching me.

We sat in the splendor of the Osteria, and he ordered the house wine as the waiter brought bread and water—*pan e coperto*—to the table. We both read through the menu, which was more elaborate than most we'd ever read, and of course, printed in Italian. After some time, Ray put his menu down. The wine arrived and the waiter poured mineral water, *acqua Fiuggi*.

"I know what I'm having," Ray said. He'd recognized the name of one dish that was the same in both Italian and English. "The carbonara."

"I need more time to decide," I said. Meanwhile, the music had started and Ray stood up, walked around to my side of the booth and bowed:

"Signorina, may I have this dance?" I rose and stood next to him, my face beaming at Ray, who was still bowing. I chortled—I was entirely ready to resuscitate one of our favorite rituals. I felt my hands get hot and prickly as he led me to the dance floor.

We danced for two numbers, moderately fast beats, finding ourselves lone dancers on the floor. Then the music switched to slow. There was an instrumental followed by a familiar Neapolitan ballad, "**Cuor' Ingrato**" or "Ungrateful Heart." The song dripped with sentiment, almost to the point of maudlin, but I loved the song. It was one I had known for years, going back to the beginning of my acting career in New York when I met and became the lover of a man who was a tenor and sang opera, including this Neapolitan love song. I started to hum the words to "*Cuor' Ingrato*," my chin on Ray's shoulder.

Our two bodies swayed, moved as one, and we paused for a few seconds at the end of each stanza. My long suppressed romantic instincts were aroused; I leaned against Ray, whispering the song's lyrics into his ear. At one point, Ray held me back from him to look deeply into my eyes: I wondered if he could see how I'd entered into an entranced state. Holding me tightly, he said: "I want you to know, hon, that I do love you."

My stomach started to pulse and I felt my gut bubbling and about to burst. I swallowed and pressed the tip of my tongue against my front teeth. I didn't want my face to give me away completely. I was afraid he would sense that I had been waiting a long time—nearly two years—to hear this. My eyes locked with his. Then I knew he knew that I had been holding back and he understood why. I turned away and lowered my head deeper into the crook of his neck as tears welled up. I thought about how romantic relationships had not come early or easily in my life. The concept of love at first sight was an experience others may have had but one I'd never known. Until Ray, I'd never even come close to having a boyfriend. Was this pattern of not feeling I belonged anywhere or to anyone about to be shed, like baby fat? Is that why in moments of insecurity I clung to Ray, because with him solidly in my life, I felt like less of an outsider?

Ray and I went back to dancing until the end of the song when the singer let out a final anguished note that was more like a gasp, the way singers end scenes in the great tragic operas. I lifted my head, faced Ray and smiled through tears of unexpected joy.

"I love you, too." *It was worth the wait.*

***

HOLIDAYS

Christmas came and went; it was a letdown. The Italians didn't make a point of shopping everywhere to find just the right thing to give every member of the family. I noticed they were immune to gift giving in general, apart from a dessert or bottle of wine, which they might bring to someone's house when invited for dinner. Exchanging gifts was a big part of Christmas for me and Ray, part of our U.S. genetic background. I marveled at the elegant and luxurious wallet he gave me, which I figured he must have gotten on a barter basis from our shopkeeper friends, Lella and Paolo. I suspected Ray did various errands and odd jobs for them in payment for whatever he acquired from their pricey boutique on the Via dei Condotti. I never brought up the subject, but I assumed that's how Ray had managed it. We bought things with cash—we didn't use credit cards in Italy; after all, this was the '70s, and we were foreigners. I got him a plush wool pullover sweater. Ray didn't wear a coat, didn't have a coat. He only had a leather jacket, and to keep warm he wore a crewneck or turtleneck underneath. Our first Christmas Eve in Rome was not spent wrapping gifts for our new friends. I felt nostalgic as I thought about December 24th only a year ago in New York when we stayed up till two in the morning wrapping presents, drinking mulled cider and listening to Christmas music. Christmas Day in Rome that first year consisted of a special afternoon meal which Armando provided just for us—*gli americani*—at the Trattoria. He served us turkey; i.e., *tacchino* with natural juices, vegetables and homemade butternut squash pasta to start. Turkey raised in Italy has a completely different taste. Their bird is smaller, the meat darker and more moist with a faintly gamey taste. *Tacchino* served by Armando at the Trattoria that Christmas was delicious, and the meal reminded us of home even if there was no cranberry sauce or pumpkin pie.

The only year-end holiday tradition we could see being practiced in Rome was *La Befana*. A vestige figure from pagan times, she was depicted as a mythical old woman with a witch's nose and carrying a broom for cleaning and sweeping. In my mind's eye I can see the bright satin puppet attire, its fabric panels flowing in the winter wind and hung in December from storefronts around the Piazza Navona. Legend has it that she comes to homes on the eve of the Epiphany (January 5th), entering through the chimney. She fills the children's socks with candy and fine presents if they've been good and she leaves coal or dark candy if they've been bad. Ray and I found out that when families expect La Befana, they leave out a small glass of wine and morsels of food. Traditionally, there is a big festival in the Piazza Navona where people assemble to look for *la befana* at midnight on the 5th of January when she is supposed to visit. Yes, there was a reason for these intriguing figures swaying around the piazza, especially from shops selling toys and candy. I was impervious to her charms, finding her mawkish. Compared to what I envisioned at this time of year—angels, nativity scenes, snowmen and reindeer—*la Befana* was austere and ugly. *No more comparisons*, an inner voice chided me. I was too homesick to listen.

New Year's Eve was also different, but at least the local Romans celebrated it. *Capo D'Anno* involved people throwing empty bottles of champagne from their windows several stories high onto the pavement below. This unrestrained partying went on as the Romans took pleasure in hearing the great crash of bottles on the sidewalks well into the wee hours of the morning. The New Year's Eve meal typically was lentils with pork belly skin—*cotechino*, among other treats, specialties generally not eaten till after 10 pm. Ray and I did not go out that night for fear of getting struck by empty bottles ejected from upper story balconies and windows of the *palazzi*.

***

GAETANO

I agonized about what to wear for my meeting with Gaetano, Umberto's journalist friend. A wool skirt and velvet jacket? Or a brown gaucho length pantsuit with brown leather boots? I chose the latter outfit, which I wore with a brown, wide-brimmed felt hat. The interview was set for 3:30 at the Trattoria, where after lunch, two waiters were scurrying to clear the tables, wipe down their tops and dust off the wood chairs and benches before setting up for the evening meal. I spotted a young man with a tiny beard sitting at a table when I walked in. He immediately rose to greet me as though he knew I was unmistakably the person he needed to meet.

"*Sono molto lieto,*" he said. (I am very pleased to meet you.) "*Cosa prendi*?" (What will you have?) He ordered two cappuccinos, and we both sat down at the table he'd staked out. Of course, I had brought my big leather portfolio of model photos and magazine clippings from my best work in New York. I lifted the book and offered it to him.

He smiled and said, "*non ancora,*" (Not just yet.) "*Ti spiego.*" (I will explain.) Gaetano had a story angle he wanted to pursue. I was to cooperate in simulating a scandal in the world of entertainment media. Being linked to a well-known figure in Italian television would force people, he reasoned, to read about someone like me who was an unknown, according to Gaetano. I kind of followed the concept, nodding in agreement when our eyes met to indicate a modicum of enthusiasm.

The two cappuccinos were placed on the table soundlessly. I instinctively started stirring the white and camel colored foam as a way of steadying my shaky hands. I was pondering the scenario he'd described in all its falseness, which was a bit unsettling. I reminded myself it would just be pretending, a minor acting bit, of sorts. *What did I have to lose,* I mused. Gaetano took out his notebook and pen. I had never been the subject of an interview with a journalist, and I found myself as apprehensive as I was thrilled. I took off my hat and put it on the chair next to me. Gaetano appeared to be only a few years older than Ray, maybe in his early '30s, and he was dressed casually chic in black slacks and a tan suede jacket. His hair was thinning, and when he smiled, his gums showed. It was a genuine smile that reassured me.

Gaetano brought up the subject of the film *Love Story*, which had done well in the U.S., and was a big hit in Italy, too, I learned.

"What are your thoughts on love versus sex as presented in the film?" he asked, using an Italian that he spoke clearly and slowly enough for me to understand.

"I've had many proposals and offers to do parts in a movie," I said. "But so far, every project involved some form of nudity. And in these particular projects, to me there was no justification for appearing nude on camera," I confided.

"What do you mean?" he asked, leaning forward with a look of concentration on his face.

"It seemed like exploitation," I said. "I don't believe we need to see sex and nudity on the screen unless it is integral to the story. That's why *Love Story*, in my mind, was such a huge success. At this time in film, we seem to be experiencing an era of sex on demand. Not that I am a prude—I oppose vulgarity. This movie is a great example of something more solid: two people really caring about one another in that *do or die* way. People crave seeing stories like that."

For the few words of English Gaetano knew, he seemed to grasp what I said. For the little Italian I spoke, sometimes resorting to English when the right Italian words didn't come to me, Gaetano listened and appeared to follow me. Was he really figuring me out, the girl who didn't want to be exploited for her body or looks? His expression was calm, his eyes reaching up into a part of his brain that was processing my comments.

"*Al loh ra*", he said, drawing out the vowel in the typical Roman manner of speaking. So then.

"Here's how I'm going to feature you. I will arrange a photo shoot with you and an upcoming television actor, a good-looking dude. All you have to do is "be seen" with him at a given time and place. I will handle the rest," he said. "And just be yourself."

"Who is this person?"

"I am not yet certain who it will be. I still have to confirm the details of the shoot. The article that comes out should appeal to people who are absorbed by every move of TV and movie actors: who they're dating, who they're cheating on, *e cosi via*, like that."

I went back to stirring my **cappuccio** (a nickname used locally) but the spoon squeaked—I was down to my last drop. He got up to go. I put my hat on and rose to walk him out. He gave me a kiss on the cheek.

The photo shoot took place the following week. I played my part, walking arm and arm with a handsome actor from Rome. Together in the rain we stared at one another as though we were in love. My fellow actor was strictly businesslike as he played his role. I supposed that he needed the exposure, too.

~ ~ ~

Long after I had given up hope that an article about me penned by Gaetano Basilici would be published, it came out, and Ray was the first to find it. It was a long interview, maybe 400 words, with photos galore of "the couple," and a separate image of only me. I gasped at how positive and favorable the content was. It acknowledged my actual credits in theater in the States and pointed out the career potential Gaetano Basilici saw for me. The reference to me as a younger version of Ali McGraw was not a main point—I was thankful for that. Who wants to be compared to another actress? He wrote that I had irresistible charm, my body was post-modern—whatever that meant! I never asked. He must have seen qualities that I guess I'd lost sight of in myself. For he wrote that I exuded a joy of life, found the noble in the crass and was at peace with myself. If I had written the article myself, I couldn't have presented a more interesting portrait. I gathered several copies of the full-page newspaper coverage, folded them and slid them into my portfolio. One day I would be glad to share what the newspaper had published. Could I now make myself believe that my fate was about to change?

***

Ciao L'Americana

LISA

In Rome, the one friend of my own choosing was another American woman about my age, Lisa. At the time, I didn't understand the need for friends, women friends especially. I made the mistake of placing too much importance on having a boyfriend and pursuing my career ambitions. It would be a lesson I needed to learn again and again throughout my life.

I met Lisa through the shopkeepers Ray and I had gotten to know. Lella and Paolo were acquainted with her as a regular customer at their luxury leather boutique on the Via dei Condotti. Lisa was married to a Roman, a writer, Luchino, whose family was wealthy. Lisa and Luchino appeared to be very much in love. I could sense an electric connection between them, which I assumed was erotic energy, and it made me envious to a degree. My intimate relationship with Ray had never been one of extreme passion. We were at home with one another, comfortable like two buddies, except one of us was male and the other female.

Lisa was a slim, leggy blonde with high cheekbones, long straight hair and pale blue eyes. Her extra height and dreamy looks qualified her as the quintessential model; modeling was what she'd done in the States. We both came from traditional families who insisted we finish college before pursuing an unconventional line of work: modeling. Our families had never given us their blessing to leave home and live in Italy. It was so gratifying to sit and talk about these things together that we started meeting for cappuccino a couple of times a week. Soft and gentle under any circumstances, Lisa sometimes acted as if she were covering something up, like a deep wound inside that nobody should see. Often she wore no makeup and had on large dark sunglasses. Lisa referred to her husband constantly, saying Luchino did this, he said that. He promised this, he accomplished that. Was the passion in their relationship also an obsession? I couldn't help wondering. When the four of us were together, Ray and I were both struck by Luchino's vivacious personality. He was animated and self-assured and he spoke perfect English, unusual among the Romans we'd come to know. He and Lisa spoke in English, which meant she had learned only about 25 Italian words. It made me question how she could get on in Italy without her husband. They had met while she was on assignment in Rome three years earlier. Whereas Ray and I were impressed by Luchino, Lisa was dazzled by him, hanging on his every word.

One day, Lisa and I met for lunch at a *tavola calda*, Italy's version of a fast-food place, except that the already cooked food is made from scratch and not packaged or processed. Once ordered, the pre-cooked dishes were reheated and served immediately. We stepped inside, and I headed across the room to a window table. Lisa hung back, moving her hand from left to right across her face to indicate that it was too bright next to the window. We settled for an inside table in a dimly lit corner.

That day as she sat down, Lisa eased into the hard back chair slowly, and then squirmed to get comfortable as though her whole body were sore. Her hands were trembling. Her eyes were obscured by over-sized dark glasses that sat low on her cheeks. I noticed her discomfort and wanted to ask her why, at the same time quieting those instincts that prompted me to ask: Did he beat you? I held back, knowing that I had an inexplicable bias against men with Luchino's incandescent charm. I suspected it was easy for men like him to prey upon vulnerable women like Lisa, isolating them, controlling them. My mind raced until I forced myself to pick up the conversation.

"Lisa, Ray and I are both pretty discouraged," I said. "This foul weather is the last thing we expected—it could almost be New York. And we are not finding work. Ray, you know, thinks he's going to put some deal together with a director."

"What do you think he might be able to do, realistically?" she asked.

"I think working for a director is a long shot. He doesn't have the experience. But I have work experience, and a resume. I feel I'm the one more likely to get work. We've both run out of money," I said in a low voice.

She nodded. Her skin, normally pale and translucent, was ashen. Maybe she hadn't slept well. Maybe they had argued, something Ray and I rarely did.

"I shouldn't be talking about my problems," I said. "How are you and Luchino doing?"

"It was a rough night." Then she was silent.

Lisa ordered a compari and soda and I asked for a *spremuta di arancia*, fresh squeezed orange juice.

"I'll tell you about it,"

"I want to know," I said. She picked up the menu and remained silent.

"What are you having?" I asked. The thought of lunch was not top of mind. When the waiter returned bearing drinks, we ordered minestrone and ravioli. I waited for her to open up about Luchino.

"No, please, you go on. It's hard for me to talk about **me**," she said as she gulped her aperitivo.

"Well, I've decided to try my luck in Milan. That's where the jobs are I've been told, in theater and fashion print work, too. Isn't that true?"

Lisa said: "It used to be, but I can't say because I stopped working when I got married. Luchino made me promise I wouldn't model anymore. He said that Italian men have dirty minds and hold little respect for girls who model. For them, models are one step up from a prostitute.

"Does he really believe that? Or did he say that to keep you from working?"

Lisa shook her head.

That is not what they'll think of me, I protested silently. How could Italy be so retrograde? It was baffling to me because in the States modeling was respectable, well-paid work. Lisa could see from the way I'd clammed up that Luchino's opinion alarmed me.

"When do you plan on going" she asked. "There is a friend, Carla, that you should meet. You'll love her."

"Next Monday."

Lisa uttered an "Oh" that seemed to come from her gut. "Is this the last time we'll see each other?" she asked, her voice growing thin and high. I detected a note of despair.

"Don't look at it that way," I said, with as little emotion as possible, not wanting to make her feel worse. "I can always come back. After all, I am leaving Ray behind."

She finished her compari and soda and searched my eyes, her elbows on the table. "Are you two breaking up?"

"No, not breaking up, but he's not coming with me," I said.

***

MILAN

Missing pieces were falling into place around my move to Milan. Yet the concept of moving there implied my never living in Rome again and no longer living with Ray. As I contemplated leaving Rome, I could not swear that I'd never be back. But Ray swore he was not leaving Rome, and would never consider moving to Milan. Being broke and out of work had diminished Ray: His spirit was shriveling. It showed in the creases around his mouth and the frown lines that deepened, it seemed, day after day. And tapping into his vulnerability heightened my own. I was struggling with the fear of being uprooted once again. I hated not having a place to call home. The thought of more tough roads to navigate without Ray unnerved me; two unmoored people were better than one, I was certain of that. A voice inside chided, "Stop whining." Hadn't I just gotten the name of someone to look up in Milan---Carla? Hadn't I just met here in Rome a *Milanese*, a young man, Giuseppe, who generously and with great enthusiasm offered to pick me up when I arrived? That meant I would eventually know at least two people in Milan and upon arrival at least, I wouldn't have to fend for myself in a bewildering train station or contend with getting a taxi.

I had met Giuseppe at Rome's Municipal Gallery of Art in Via Cagliari, not far from Armando's trattoria. We were both staring at the featured artist's depiction of the Piazza Vittorio Veneto. Giuseppe must have assumed I was there because I love the work of Giorgio de Chirico, a reasonable assumption, although I was not an art follower at the time. He had struck up a conversation by commenting to me that De Chirico was on permanent exhibit at one of Milan's galleries. I then told him I was moving to Milan for work purposes and I was very excited about it.

"When is it you are traveling, and are you taking the train?" he asked in Italian.

"I leave on February 10th, a Monday, in the afternoon. Yes, on the train," I said.

"I would be happy to pick you up unless you already have someone coming for you," he said.

"No, not at all. I have no friends in Milan. I don't know anyone yet. I only know of a model agency there affiliated with my New York agency." I was counting on the agency getting me decent jobs. If they sent me on assignments that paid even half as much as in New York, it would be enough, for a while anyway, I thought. "So, I am hoping things work out," I said.

Giuseppe, by my reckoning, was about 30, slim, wearing black jeans and a black knit, long sleeved top. He had pale skin, brown eyes and thick wavy brown hair. His features were delicate and refined. There was an air of confidence and finesse about him. He had *sprezzatura*, what the Italians would define as the ability to pull off what you did with elegance and ease, as though it were effortless, a behavior widely displayed and greatly admired.

"*Senti*." Listen, Ruth. I will pick you up and then we'll go to dinner. I would be pleased to act as an unofficial host. Milano is my home town," he said.

"You are so kind—*molto gentile. Va bene*. I thank you."

"Here is my phone number," he said, taking out a card. "Give me a call two days before you leave and let me know exactly what time you arrive. I will be at the station," he said.

Ray took me to the station and loaded my luggage on the train, marking my place by laying down my garment bag. Feeling nervous about boarding, I gave him a thumb's up. The conductor was announcing in a deep voice and heavy Roman accent that passengers were kindly requested to board. Ray and I hugged, and saying goodbye choked me up—it felt so final. I told him I'd call that night. He hugged me again and helped me up the stairs into the car. I settled myself by the window and looked out as the train pulled away. In that moment I thought I'd never see him again. I waved out the window. He gave me a thumb's up. I sank down into a hard seat and closed my eyes, feeling very alone, disturbed by self-doubts and self-pity. Where was my courage?

My disquiet was preempted hours later by the startling impact of arriving at the Milan train station. I felt swallowed up in its cavernous space. The buzz of people and the noise of trains tunneling in coupled with the stench of overheated metal grinding to a halt every two minutes made me almost dizzy. In general, train stations caused me to imagine falling off the platform into the pit. People strode by me, moving fast and with purpose. I moved slowly, barely managing to guard my baggage while looking around to see if Giuseppe had shown up. I could see nothing or nobody familiar. Suddenly, there he was.

"*Ciao, ciao. Sei arrivata*" (You arrived), he said, as though it were an accomplishment. He smiled and grazed my cheek with a kiss, Italian style. Then he grabbed the large suitcases and flung my garment bag over his arm. All I had left to carry was a small valise and my make up case. He led me nimbly outside, where he had pulled his car up to the curb, probably in a no parking zone. He put my suitcases in the trunk of the car with my make up case and lay the garment bag on the back seat. Once at the wheel driving toward the city center, he said: "*Come ti senti? Sei stanca?*" (Are you tired? How do you feel?)

"Not at all, I feel fine. I am *su di giri* (over the moon) to be in

Milano. And you are so sweet to come for me." I reminded myself how fortunate I was to be in the company of someone as endearing as Giuseppe, and yet he was a virtual stranger. I hadn't been alone in the presence of any man except Ray in years, and I felt mildly disloyal to Ray. As I unbuttoned my long leather coat and settled into the front seat, I enjoyed being driven somewhere in a private car, not a taxi.

"*Ai fame?*" (Are you hungry?) Giuseppe asked.

"Yes, I'm hungry. I forgot to have lunch."

Giuseppe took us to a typical Milanese restaurant: noisy, crowded with diners and staffed with cordial, highly skilled waiters who took pride in taking a food order and then serving savory dishes with sweeping gestures and predictable panache. The proprietor and the waiters greeted Giuseppe as though they knew him well, yet the familiarity was respectful in every way. I sensed Giuseppe and his family had some standing, possibly from good lineage or accumulated wealth. He gave off the aura of someone untroubled about such things as work, a roof over your head, the cost of eating in a fine restaurant. He appeared at ease in his own skin, at age 30. Maybe that is why he wanted to help—he was concerned about my plight.

"So much is at stake," I said, trying to explain to him in Italian the complexity of my situation with words that eluded me. So, I said simply: "*Ho molto da fare.*" (I have a lot to do.) "And I want to work in Milano. I also need to work. Rome, I found, had very few work opportunities."

He nodded. "Yes, I agree. It is not a city of opportunities. It is the center of bureaucracy, a government town, and inefficient at that" he said. "I would like to know if I could help in some way," he said, as we walked out of the restaurant toward the car, he, of course, walking on the street side of me. His manner appeared very sincere, warm, but not overly friendly. Standing next to the car, about to open the door, he noticed that the triangle shaped window on the driver's side had been smashed. His car had been broken into. The trunk had been popped as well. We saw that my suitcases and the garment bag were gone. The only thing the thieves had not taken was my trunk case containing toiletries and cosmetic paraphernalia.

"*Mi dispiace,*" (I am so sorry), he said.

I couldn't say anything. My things were stolen, an event not tragic enough to cry about, but one that filled me with a sense of doom. Was this the price to pay for venturing out, for taking a chance? I felt a sharp pain across my shoulders. I reached my hand around and rubbed the back of my neck—my head felt so heavy I could not hold it up straight. I began muttering to myself in English:

"How can I look for work with no clothes to my name? What will I do?" Then out loud in Italian: I said, "Giuseppe, this is a bad sign. All my things, gone! It means I may have bad luck in Milano. *Niente di fortuna qui.*"

"Please don't think that," he said quickly. "*Niente affatto.* (It's not bad luck.) "This is only one incident. Car burglary is very common in Milan. I should have known better than to leave the car on the street instead of with an attendant in a parking lot. It is my fault," he said.

***

GIUSEPPE

Not your fault, my fault. The thought echoed in my mind. *It was a mistake to come here at all, and this proves it,* I told myself. I grabbed the belt to my leather coat by the ends and retied it around my waist. Then I sat down on the sidewalk, my hands cupping my ears. I was losing it. Staring at the ground, I said: "*Si. Uno sbaglio*—a mistake. I am left with nothing, not even clothes."

"No, not a mistake," Giuseppe said, in a new voice, loud and agitated, causing me to look up. His face, once so joyful about welcoming me to Milan, now appeared stricken, as if he felt he'd hurt me far more than helped me. "Please," he said, extending his hands to pull me to my feet. "Tell me how much your things were worth."

"What do you mean?" I asked, still dazed.

"I mean if you tell me how much you lost, in dollars more or less, I will give you that amount," Giuseppe said, his voice more even now, having hit upon a solution, one that he thought would be fair.

"I don't know. I have to think about it," I said. "Right now, I can't think."

"Because I am responsible for your loss and it is only right that I repay you—I will do that, maybe by tomorrow. I feel so terrible for you. May I please offer you a place to stay tonight—at my apartment?" Giuseppe asked.

Giuseppe was testing the limits of my ability to trust men. I had a deep-rooted fear of men taking advantage of me, saying pretty things to get into my pants, or to cajole me into taking drugs and then seduce me. Like many fears, mine weren't always justified. I had always managed to avoid being abused or exploited. I looked away in embarrassment that he thought I would accept such a proposal.

"Don't worry, you have the guest room all to yourself. Tomorrow we'll have lunch at my place, too. The servants prepare a nice meal. By the end of our lunch, I hope to have the money to repay you," he said.

I looked closely at Giuseppe. He was decidedly not the sleazy type. And I had detected he came from wealth from our first encounter in the art gallery. His eyes were entreating me—his body language was respectful, his voice tender, as though beseeching me to let him make good on this mishap.

"But how can I be sure that you don't want something from me? I have a boyfriend in Rome and he's not with me now. But we've been together a long time," I said.

Giuseppe drew himself to his full height and gazed straight at me, standing tall and resolute.

"I haven't asked you for anything," he said firmly. "I don't want anything from you," as if to suggest that I had been the one with evil thoughts.

That reassured me.

His residence was in a late 19th century building. It felt large, its walls of rooms extending from one side to the other in the manner of a full floor residence with the living room at the center. My room could have been a guest bedroom. It had a double sized, puffy bed with a comforter and duvet, rows of matching fabric pillows, graceful figurine porcelain lamps, a draped night table and its own bathroom. The living room—the salon—was traditional period European décor: heavy drapery, carved wood framed sofas, shiny dark wood surfaces on tables, settees and sideboards. Looking around the guest room, I saw a phone and asked Giuseppe if I could use it to call Rome.

"Of course. Help yourself, and let me know if you need anything else. I will see you tomorrow for *il pranzo* (lunch)," he said, and shut the door behind him. A minute later he knocked and came back in. "I just want to know what your things that were stolen were worth," he said once again in extra clear Italian.

"Maybe about $400," I said slowly, still adding up numbers. It was an amount that would be equivalent to three times as much money by today's currency standards.

"*Va bene*," he said. "See you tomorrow."

I dialed the number of the Tratttoria in Rome, hoping Ray would still be there at almost 11 o'clock; I was relieved when Armando brought Ray to the phone. After I explained what happened, Ray said: "You should have been more careful, hon. You have to watch out. Milan is a big city."

"I know, I know. But it happened. What you just said doesn't make me feel any better."

"I'm sorry, hon. I really am. I know how much this move means to you, but just be careful, will you? Maybe it's the only bad thing that will ever happen to you in Milan."

"I'm so tired, and right now I just want to go to sleep and forget it all ever happened. I wish you were here," I told him. I hung up, feeling that in my worst moment, I had no one.

The next day, I was still shaken and my stomach was queasy; the burglary and the strangeness of the circumstances were unsettling. The surroundings, although luxurious, were not familiar and rather formal. I got dressed and somehow managed to find the kitchen, where there was some coffee left on the stove. It was late in the morning. I had the sense I wasn't the only one in the home, although I didn't see anyone and Giuseppe was nowhere to be found. I helped myself to coffee and went back to the room to get ready. I applied my makeup carefully, taking time to cover the dark circles from a fitful night's sleep, grateful that the thieves had not taken my make up case.

Giuseppe politely knocked on my door around 1:00 and asked if I was ready for lunch. The two of us sat at a small dining table by the window to enjoy a three-course meal served on platters that had been placed before he called me in. The meal was obviously the work of servants, but they were behind the scenes—I never saw them. I wondered if Giuseppe had planned it that way. Maybe he thought seeing his servants would spook me, an American presumably raised differently. The thought crossed my mind. We finished our meal with an espresso and a slice of fruit tarte for dessert.

"Giuseppe, what an elegant meal. Thank you so much. Your hospitality is much appreciated and you've been so *gentile*. I hope you don't think I'm the kind of girl who normally spends the night at a stranger's house. In fact, I don't know what kind of person you really think I am," I said, suddenly feeling stripped of dignity, hating being so beholden.

He waved away my concern, saying: "*Niente affatto,*" (not in the least.) "But I want to put things to rest and do the right thing," he said. We had moved to the living room. Giuseppe told me he'd gone to the bank and gotten the money in American dollars in denominations he thought would be easily negotiated. "*Per non crearti problemi.*" (So that you won't have a problem.) He must have wisely assumed that I had no bank account. He handed me four $100 bills. I thanked him. He seemed pleased, and his shoulders went up and down as he heaved a big sigh of relief.

"*Va bene.* You can stay as long as you like this afternoon."

"Thank you anyway. It is time for me to find the hotel where I will stay for a while until I get my own place. Obviously, it won't be as nice as this," I said looking around one last time.

He walked me downstairs to the street. I thanked him again and squeezed his hand. I had never known such impeccable behavior on the part of a man. Was it breeding, was it kindness, was it the Italian way, or was Giuseppe a jewel of a person? And in spite of the theft, wasn't I lucky it happened with Giuseppe, who had been my unanticipated knight. He helped me into a taxi, leaving his hand on the closed door.

"*Mi raccomando,*" he said, speaking with authority and handing *lire* to the driver to ensure that he would drop me off safely at the Hotel Torino.

***

BREAK-UP

Oh, how I struggled to rid myself of the gnawing sense of being damned for having left Rome—and Ray—venturing out on my own to start a career in Milan. The car break-in and theft of my luggage, coupled with Giuseppe's involvement, had shown me that I couldn't relax in the presence of an Italian man, no matter how well behaved and generous. Lunch with Giuseppe at his home was an uneasy experience; I'd felt a chasm between us. For Giuseppe understood virtually no English, and my fledgling Italian didn't allow the ideal communication. How could we penetrate the barriers that guarded our separate lives? I missed the familiarity and stability of Ray, whose ambivalence about my move also made me doubt myself. Beyond the fear of striking out on my own, I was feeling a crippling loneliness.

The room they gave me in the hotel was simple, but a bit more up to date than Olga's studio rental in Rome. At least it had a hot plate and a mini fridge, which made it possible for me to take meals in the room instead of eating alone in a restaurant. I immediately took to the Italian way of grocery shopping. It was an adventure to visit the cheese and fruit stalls, counters that sold ham and prosciutto—all unpackaged, measured out for purchase in grams rather than ounces. Food shopping, *fare la spesa*, would oblige me to calculate amounts in the metric system. And it required me to speak Italian.

The next step was to get some clothes to make up for my stolen wardrobe. Fiorucci, I found was Milan's least traditional, boldest fashion department store and the most affordable, given the stylishness of its clothing. I bought two skirts, a pair of boots and a sweater. I wanted to make sure I had the right look for my initial visit the next morning to the model agency, Giorgio Piazzi.

They received me in a routine, businesslike manner, but not unfavorably. After all, to them I was just another model looking for work. They told me they'd put me to work as soon as they had need for talent. Meanwhile, I took the names of several photographers they recommended and resolved to call on them to ask for test shots.

Test shots are photos that a professional photographer agrees to take without charge: the model gives her time and talent in exchange for photos, and during the photo shoot the photographer often experiments with a new lens or a new technique. The best shots of face and fashion then go into my portfolio. I had taken test shots in New York City. In Rome, the well-known photographer Pier Luigi had shot me in his enormous white studio, where the walls displayed images of Italian celebrities, including photos of the actress Verna Lisi. In Milan, I eventually managed to call on a German photographer whose work was strikingly different, as was he. A true eccentric, he had wild, thinning, frizzy gray hair, a scrawny build and a no-nonsense manner. Would he have any interest in shooting with me? There was no way to predict. He agreed to a photo session the following week. During the shoot he hardly spoke except to show me how he wanted me to hold my head and place my chin. I took an instant liking to his prints, taken from the neck up, using black and white flush soft focus on the close-ups. His lens had bared a dreamy and vulnerable expression, and evoked in me a sensual yet veiled presence behind the piercing dark eyes. The images were arresting, not at all mundane, and I was proud enough to include them in my portfolio.

By the end of the week, the agency had booked me on a job doing catalog fashion work. Think the equivalent of JC Penny in Italy. Nobody wanted to do catalog work, it was not dynamic or artistic. Yet it would be a start in a new city, and it meant getting a paycheck. About three weeks later, I went to the agency to collect it. By now, I had grown to enjoy going to the agency, which was not sterile like an office, but flooded with natural light and configured with a sizable open space for clients to congregate. I always heard various languages spoken, and often ran into people from other European countries as well as the States, who had come on a special assignment to shoot on location in Italy.

That day, the staff gave me a written message. It was from Ray, and he was asking me to call him. I hadn't even suspected that he was in Milan. I called him, and was stunned to hear him say that he'd left Rome "for good." He didn't mention when he'd arrived in Milan. We had a stilted conversation, and I found him to be cool and evasive. I already was irritated that he might be using my modeling agency as a springboard to get work for himself. I suppressed my rising annoyance as he got to the point.

"Listen, there's going to be an important presentation on Scientology that you'll be interested in," he said.

"On what? Really. When did you hook up with the Scientology people, Ray? I am surprised you never let me know you were coming to Milan. How long have you been here for God's sake," trying to hide my hurt and feeling a sense of betrayal all over again.

"Not long. About a week," he said. "The people here who are involved in Scientology are first rate. I'm blown away by them."

"When is the presentation and where?" I asked halfheartedly, not feeling the pull to attend that Ray clearly felt.

"Tomorrow night at 7 o'clock, right here in the agency. Do you remember Jane Hitchcock?"

"Of course, I do. She is or was one of the top models, on cover after cover, represented by Wilhelmina, my affiliate agency in New York."

"Well," he said, "she's in the Scientology group," as though to prove his point.

Giving in, I said. "OK, OK, I'll come. And maybe we could have dinner afterward."

"Well, let's see how long it goes, and if they have anything planned for after the meeting. There should be at least one big wig from Scientology's European division here."

What had gotten into Ray, I wondered. Had he found a new cause, something to believe in? Or was he just being swayed and taken in by the celebrity aspect, the first-rate nature—to use his language—of those he'd been meeting?

I showed up the next night and sat in one of the folding chairs set up in the agency's large waiting room. Ray seemed unconcerned with where I sat; he was helping to set up easels with large sheets of paper on which appeared to be information about the group's practices and principals, in large enough print that I could read it from my seat in the back. There were fewer than twelve people in the room, and at least three of them were in front managing the presentation. I read a blurb calling it a religion, another describing Scientology as a technology developed by L. Ron Hubbard. Still another easel stated that **Man's Capabilities Are Unlimited**.

Two people spoke who sounded strong and energetic, but their tone was insistent. They repeated themselves a lot and spoke as though this set of principles was the only concept that a person could abide by to be fully realized. To me, they were so high spirited that they left no space for reflecting and savoring the ideas they put forth. Afterwards, Ray said to me: "What'dya think?"

"I don't know. It sounds very strict to me, like a religion without a church." As a one-time Catholic who never intended to go back to church, I hated the insistence on believing in only one true path. Besides that, I had majored in psychology at university and firmly believed in psychotherapy, which included some of the theories of Freud and Jung. Scientology promoted its own theories and maintained that trained volunteers could help people improve and achieve their goals.

"I don't know, Ray. How do you view it?"

"I think they're onto something. Look at this list of people who've completed the program and how successful they are," he said, holding up one of the handouts. I skimmed it and nodded, handing it back. Ray looked disappointed.

"The local director pretty much recruited me to do their intensive training. They told me they would waive all fees if I agree to start with them right away. I would go on to teach the program after that."

"And you agreed? What is the commitment?"

"It's indefinite. I mean it has no finish date. For as long as I want," he said.

I shifted my weight from one foot to the other, my stomach buzzing with a revulsion I couldn't attribute to anything but a sense of danger that was engulfing me.

"Ray, I don't think this is for me." I said slowly. I had admitted it, yet I felt no relief.

He looked at me, and his expression was frozen, his face white. Had he hoped for a positive response, and why did it matter?

"Well, it's a given that you be into this with me or we don't have a future," Ray said.

I was shocked by his decision to sever our relationship. I was wounded by his throwing it away for something new and trendy, still not well known. What kind of a person puts a relationship on the line if their partner doesn't buy into a cultish, still largely unproven program like Scientology? I quickly put on my coat and tied the belt, lifting my purse to my shoulder. *Don't worry about me. I can make it on my own.* I took a breathy breath. "You're right. We are over." I turned around and headed blindly toward the exit, my heart praying that Ray and I would never run into one another again.

I still had a lump in my throat an hour later when I got to my hotel room. As I replayed the words of our conversation, I could see his face, as pale as a lily, the dark circles under his eyes, his physique, thinner than usual, and his nervous hands, smoking furiously. He hadn't allowed for even a moment of loving reunion, and although the abrupt ending was a shock, I realized there was no longer anything holding us together.

***

ANTONIO

The agency continued to send me on bread-and-butter assignments, resulting in photos that wound up inside fashion catalogs, not on the cover of fashion magazines. These jobs were steady initially, and they earned me enough money to leave the tawdry Hotel Torino in the urban heart of Milan. Using Giuseppe's cash reimbursement, I'd paid for the hotel and bought clothes. I saved money by avoiding restaurants—no fun eating alone in any case. I often finagled invitations from people I met to be their guest for dinner. The Italians took to me. Was it my being in thrall with all things Italian, my curiosity to learn about all things Italian? Or was I just "different" enough to intrigue them? Sharing a meal was an ingrained gesture of hospitality, and rarely did I decline the invitation, even from those who were brand new. I can't remember the many ways I met them, but it was clear I had a knack for attracting people, both women and men, all of whom appeared to be well bred and sincere. On a social level, I was succeeding.

Luckily, I stumbled upon a studio to rent that required no elaborate references nor a security deposit. It was in a newer apartment hotel called La Residence (Ray zee dahnse) offering furnished units. Mine had a living area separated by a wall from the bedroom, which was wholly occupied by a king-sized bed, replete with bed linens, blinds, drapes and thick mocha colored carpeting. At one end of the small living room (*salotto*) was a large window, and at the other an electric stove, refrigerator and sink that faced a round glass dining table. The building had an expansive lobby with a couch and chairs, and off to one side were elevators leading to the residences. The focal point of the grand lobby was a concierge desk with an all-day concierge who officiously greeted visitors and called up the resident to announce a caller. It was gratifying that my neighbors were single, about my age, Italian, and almost all were graduate students studying for a business master's degree at the nearby la Bocconi University. The only inconvenience was that La Residence at Via Momigliano 2 was on the periphery of Milan, and food markets, gift shops and clothing stores were far away. My commute anywhere, including for job interviews, invariably meant a long tram ride. And the tram it was because a taxi was too costly now that I had rent to pay. It was my good fortune, too, that the gallantry of the Italian man would lead him to brave the heavy city traffic to the periphery, where he would pick me up at my address to take me out for dinner. The concierge would announce my date, and I never had to be concerned about a new person coming inside or entering my space, truly too intimate for visitors. I enjoyed the security of the fortress-like building, and gradually began to relax. I eventually could put aside anxious thoughts of car burglaries and fears of being followed walking along the side streets, which had plagued me for weeks at the Hotel Torino, admittedly in the wrong part of town.

Through a brand-new person, Franca Chizzoli, whom I befriended at a party, I was introduced to a man. Antonio was an educated, working professional, who was about my age, and he had moved to Milan from Bari, a major city located on the Adriatic coast in the southeastern region of *Le Puglie, aka Puglia*. He spoke with a southern Italian accent, which sounded refined and dignified, and his deep voice wooed me. I found him easy to listen to, his resonant speech soothing and so unlike the nasal, whining sound coming from the local *Milanesi*, whose accent to me was unpleasant. After first hearing Romans speak their version of Italian—expressive and sardonic—it struck me that the whirring Milanese accent was as destructive to the mellifluous sound of proper Italian as a thick Bronx accent was to the cultivated accent of someone bred in the well-schooled circles of the Northeastern U.S. Although I was still learning Italian, I was able to hear the difference in the sounds and could distinguish accents among people from various localities, feeling blessed that I had a good ear.

Antonio stood in refreshing contrast to anyone I had ever been attracted to, beginning with his appearance. He was about my height, maybe an inch or so taller, and his physique was borderline skinny. He had pronounced cheek bones, a deep olive complexion and dark eyes that brimmed with a brooding awareness. In spite of the fact that he resembled some of my uncles who also hailed from the Adriatic Coast (*Abbruzze-Molise*) and whom I had considered homely, I didn't find Antonio unpleasant to look at, even with his mildly bulbous nose. For work, he was required to wear a dark suit. Not one that he wore fit him properly, the shoulder pads hanging off his small frame and sleeves cascading below his wrists. In his rumbling voice—somewhat raspy from smoking—he spoke very deliberately, fixing his eyes on me. His presentation was earnest and direct. Unlike Ray, he wasn't clowning or inflating his tales all the time. To my delight, I could understand everything he said.

One day, I picked up my mail to find something from an entirely unexpected sender: the Department of Immigration and Foreign Residency. The envelope bore a seal and stamp markings that indicated a possible summons, government generated. I opened it with unsteady hands and read it, trying to make sense of the technical Italian language, incomprehensible to me. One word popped out: *Denuncia*. Had I inexplicably been turned in for a random act or deed? By whom? When? I saw one other word I recognized; Positano. Positano? That's where I'd done my first job last December: the comedy skit modeling designer fashion clothing. I felt nauseous at the thought of repercussions from what had brought so much pride and excitement. I soon realized that I needed an interpreter and an advisor. I held off showing the notification to Antonio, afraid that he'd want nothing more to do with me, a foreigner who may have also gotten into trouble with the law. Dreading the possible outcome if I didn't protect myself, I brought it up to two acquaintances, both lawyers. Each one shrugged it off with the sort of disdain for rules that I would come to see as typical of the Italian spirit. The Italians bend the rules; witness the way they form—or don't form—a line in public, to give only one example. My lawyer buddies didn't see the official missive as a threat to my daily life nor did they see me as being at fault. One of them offered a temporary solution, which was to drive me across the Italian Swiss border to get my passport stamped by the Swiss authorities. They informed me that this would legalize my stay, at least in the short term. Each of them urged me not to worry and pointed out there was a time frame for responding. The news made my heart pound, I was crushed that I had to deal with another calamity just as I was settling in—it seemed cruel. A voice within wailed, what could I possibly have done wrong? Part of my discomfort was due to not having anyone to turn to for a permanent solution. My common sense led me to consult Antonio, even if he wound up scolding me or, worse yet, abandoning me. After all, he worked in the department of *Questura*. Questura, in a small country like Italy, provided many services. Beyond serving as police headquarters, it handled passport processing, public relations, immigration, fraud protection, domestic violence and elder abuse cases. He worked in the Office of Relations with the Public located in Via Fatebenefratelli, which had the longest hours of any department, from 8 a.m. to 2 p.m. and 4 p.m. to 7 p.m. These long hours dealing with the public was something he always lamented. Surely, he was qualified to give me advice.

The next night when we got together, I showed Antonio the summons. I saw him sink into a chair and study it with intense concentration. He raised his hand, angling his wrist as he held up the summons, blowing out a breath that I read as exasperation or exhaustion or both.

"Can you explain the problem? Who is denouncing me and why," I asked. Antonio was silent and I could sense he wanted to choose his words carefully before answering.

"I don't know," he said. My temple began to throb, my face became flushed, and I was squeezing my hands uncontrollably.

"Please understand that this is serious," he said still holding up the paper. "Very serious." I nodded, speechless, barely able to breathe. We stared at each other.

"You may have to leave the country. Depending on what is decided on the deportation matter. It may be for good, never to return again," he said solemnly. Placing his hands on my shoulders, his eyes big and round: "How did you get yourself into this mess?"

**

COURT

"How did you get yourself into this mess?" he asked again, coming closer and peering into my face. Specifically, he said the commonly used word *casino*, meaning mess, as in trouble or disaster. I couldn't give him a proper answer, so I proceeded to tell him what had happened in Positano.

"Some months ago, while I was living in Rome, I accepted a modeling job through an agency in Naples."

"*A Napoli?*" He asked this with discernible alarm. Antonio fixed his searching eyes on me as though I were a naughty child instead of a 27-year-old girl who was living on her own in a new country. He normally acted with serenity and a savoir faire beyond his 29 years, something I liked about him. Now he appeared agitated as he waited for more of my account.

"The job came from the head of a local talent and model agency, a man connected to a designer who was launching a clothing line. I never thought there was anything wrong in working. Why would they have hired me if they didn't have the right to do so?"

Antonio sat down on the velour couch in my living room and rested his chin on his hand.

"What did I do wrong?" I asked. "I never even got paid."

"The Neapolitans do things their way, *a sua manera*," he said, as if to explain everything. "You don't know anything about Naples, do you?" He lowered his head, giving the impression he didn't want me to see him as he deciphered the situation. Then he flicked his cigarette in the ashtray on the coffee table, stamping it out half smoked.

"*E grave*. This is serious. You could be in huge trouble with the law. They may well have grounds to deport you."

"And here I am in Italy, the Italy I love," I said, my voice trembling and then breaking. I was sitting at the far end of the couch, away from Antonio, who seemed remote. I felt shut out, isolated and alone in my dilemma. Some part of me saw this summons as another sign that my plan to settle in Italy was being thwarted. It was another blow, just like the car break-in and the loss of all my things on my first night in Milan. How many times could I call it bad luck? Maybe I was cursed.

"Can't you help me? I've no one else to turn to, Antonio, and I trust you more than anybody I've met so far."

"*Ci sto pensando, veramente*," he said. (I'm thinking. I'm thinking hard.)

I took his hand in mine. Antonio didn't speak for what felt like an hour, not a few minutes.

"I have a good friend, Salvatore, a trial lawyer. I will explain your situation to him and ask if he will accept the case. But you may have to pay him."

I nodded, taking his hand to my lips and kissing it. Paying for a lawyer would be impossible. I barely made ends meet after the rent was paid every month. The modeling jobs had gradually dried up and I was now teaching English at Berlitz, certainly not earning any more than what helped to buy groceries. I prayed that Antonio's friend would not expect payment. I was becoming desperate.

I didn't miss the irony in knowing that *Salvatore*, his friend's name, meant savior. He was the same age as Antonio, about the same height, but with his stocky build, he looked short. Salvatore had thick hair worn slicked down off a generous forehead, high cheekbones and a strong nose that complimented the alert way he held his head as though lifted out of his neck. He stood erect, shoulders squared off, in a stance that was poised and effusive at the same time, with a touch of swashbuckling. In fact, he seemed too young to embody so fully the demeanor of an authoritarian figure and trusted advisor. Although I didn't realize it at the time, he was still a kid—he and Antonio and I were all kids, doing our first jobs, working at our first careers. Like Antonio, he spoke with a heavy Southern Italian accent, articulating in a rather formal way.

Salvatore told me that out of his friendship with Antonio—they had been classmates in law school—he would take my case. There was no mention of a fee. I squeezed his forearm and smiled weakly in gratitude. He immediately set up a verbal timetable, saying he would start work on it right away and get ready to represent me in court, in *tribunale*, as he called the courtroom. The trial needed to take place by a certain deadline, a mere three weeks away,

"You will take the stand," he told me. Just when I thought he had come to my rescue, I was jolted to hear that I needed to appear in court. I felt as if a bucket of ice-cold water had been thrown at me. I was filled with a terror I had never known.

But why? I felt inadequate to speak to a judge. What if I got trapped and confused in ignorance of the proper way to answer. What would happen then?

"Salvatore, *ti prego*," I beg you, I said over and over. "Please don't let me stand before a judge. I will be ridiculed by someone in authority who wants me punished."

That familiar voice inside hounded me. How would they view me: a girl, a foreigner, whose work record consisted of a modeling job in Naples, done as they said, illegally? How would these men judge me, an American, a single woman who was not living with parents and living moreover far from home? The court might not understand at all that I was trying to survive and my actions were the result of my desire to remain in the country. Would they realize that I sought to be accepted by the culture, not to violate its rules and offend its social mores?

"I don't want to get up and be questioned. I don't want to take the stand in court," I blurted out loudly.

"*Non ti preoccupare*" (Don't worry), he said. He insisted that my participation would actually help me. He was convinced that his strategy was the right defense.

On the day of the trial, Antonio had to work and was unable to accompany me. I had bubbles in my stomach when I arrived in the lobby of the court building. I'd worn one of my more sedate outfits: the brown gaucho pant suit with brown leather boots and a matching felt hat. Feeling no air in my lungs, my short quick breaths were robbing me of calm. I wanted to hide my face under the wide brim of my hat and have it be over. Was I going to lose everything I'd created for myself during my fourteen months in Italy? I had put together the foundation of a more stable life. I'd left modeling and found a suitable and legal job teaching English as a second language. I was creating a circle of friends who hosted me, instructed me and showed me local historic treasures, included gastronomic haunts over long weekend treks. I'd even managed to arrange free Italian lessons with a graduate student who graciously held rigorous conversation with me in exchange for a *caffe latte*. Would I be stripped of all of this?

Still waiting outside the court, I couldn't sit, nor could I stand still. I paced back and forth, back and forth across the marble floor. Salvatore arrived and greeted me with a happy smile and open arms, leading me into the courtroom. His self-assurance and warmth gave me no comfort. The only way I could overcome the dread of taking the stand was to pretend this whole event really wasn't happening to me but to someone whom I was observing. I tried to distance myself from my actual experience. I watched Salvatore closely.

As he stood before the judge, looking taller than he was, he seemed powerful, his shoulders spread wide under his double-breasted suit. I can almost hear him now, his musical voice saying things about me that I couldn't entirely translate while his hands moved and his chest expanded in attempt to convey my blamelessness. As he spoke with remarkable energy and a strong voice, he turned to me as he finished his comments and then he sat down. The judge called me to the stand and asked that I identify myself and give my current address. The Judge did not ask me to speak further. He spoke. Using a somber tone, he asked me to unconditionally agree not to repeat the same activity or make the same mistake.

"Si," I said emphatically.

He warned me that a second offense would be beyond reparation—unpardonable—and he asked if I understood those consequences.

"I do, your Honor," I replied in Italian.

The Judge pounded the gavel. "Case dismissed."

I was exonerated. Salvatore came over to me and we walked out together. He shook my hand. His forehead was shining with perspiration and his cheeks were hot and moist when I brushed them with a kiss. He placed his two hands on my shoulders and looked at me solemnly.

"*Sei stata fortunata.*" You were lucky, Ruth. He smiled, and I thanked him, feeling drained, if not relieved, but for the cramps in my stomach which had absorbed all the fear and anxiety of the trial.

"I owe you my life, Salvatore, my life in Italy."

That night when Antonio came over, he was less uptight. He reaffirmed what Salvatore had said about my being fortunate, adding that he wouldn't be able to get me out of any such mess a second time. I was contrite, reassuring him I had learned a hard lesson and would never again make the same mistake.

"I owe my being able to stay in Italy to you and Salvatore."

I could feel Antonio relaxing at last as he sat close to me on the couch. Seeing his softened face and meeting the steady gaze of his shiny eyes, I could tell that he had never blamed me. I sensed he'd come to accept me as both naïve and adventurous and above all, different from most of the women in his country. I was someone seeking new experiences, even if it turned out to be risky.

* * *

CARLA

I did call Carla, Lisa's friend. After our conversation, half in English on her part and half in Italian on my part, she enthusiastically said she would love to meet me and would put something together: dinner in a restaurant outside of Milan and, of course, she would pick me up. She came with her date and a date for me. The Italians were inclined to make a foursome out of a threesome, comfortable in a world of couples. Carla had ingeniously pulled out two men from her home town of Erba, a suburb of Como, which meant they could all ride into Milan together. As a bonus, the two men could speak English. I was thrilled at the prospect of developing a new woman friend. She and I sat en route in the tight quarters of the back seat of an Alfa Romeo Grande. When we turned toward each other, I could feel her knees touching mine, and it made me smile broadly.

"Very pleased to meet you," she said with a boyish grin that showed straight white teeth and healthy gums. Her face was less Italian than Austrian: straight nose, hazel eyes, short dirty blonde hair. She spoke in a low voice with a marked pronunciation of her words.

"*Il piacere e mio,*" (the pleasure is all mine) I said, remembering the frequently used phrase, almost an alternative to saying thank you.

"Oh, you speak Italian," one of the men said in Italian, piping up from the passenger seat. The younger one, who wasn't driving, turned around to catch my eye.

"I just know a few phrases, and you'll hear me saying the same

Ciao L'Americana

ones again and again.," I laughed. "But I want to learn to speak Italian like you. *Forse.*" (Maybe.) "Soon, I hope," I said in Italian.

I didn't want to be the kind of American who was unable to adapt to local customs and learn the local language, so I always made the effort to express myself in Italian, no matter how frustrating, given my limited vocabulary. If the men did speak English, as Carla said, I wasn't hearing English roll off their tongues. As we drove along, they were exchanging comments in Italian that I couldn't grasp at all. Their accent was unfamiliar, and it was a different cadence from the Italian spoken in Rome. Maybe they were speaking in dialect. Carla and I chatted briefly about Lisa, my experience in Rome, and what made me decide to come to Italy.

"Well, I'd like to live here permanently—I just love it," I said.

"*Si si si. Che bello.*" (Yes. How lovely)

We had left the *autostrada* and were plying a route that appeared to lead out of the city, where the trees arched over the avenue and the traffic diminished. Their car pulled into a circular driveway and stopped in front of an awning. Carla and I were helped out by a valet attendant. While our two dates gathered their jackets and purses and tipped the attendant, Carla and I stood together, and I surveyed her admiringly, imagining her as a future role model.

"*Brava, Carla,*" I said, looking around and noticing the carpet leading to the posh entrance. I was attempting to express that I approved of the way she'd managed to have both of us taken out to a tony place. She laughed at the compliment and said, "*Ho combinato bene,*" (Yes, I put it together. I wanted you to enjoy)

Her date was the older of the two men. A native of Como, he was a ruggedly handsome man of about 55 with salt and pepper hair and a soft voice. His name was Primo: Primo for first, the firstborn of the family. Carla was tall, nearly Primo's height and at 34, she was about 20 years younger than Primo and only a little older than the other man, Ambrogio, the one who was my dinner date. According to Carla, Ambrogio was a favorite employee of Primo's, and the two men acted like buddies in spite of their differences in rank and age. Although Primo had sons working at the textile plant, he had delegated considerable authority to Ambrogio. Carla told me they were often out together, both socially and on business.

I discovered that Carla was seeing Primo even though she knew he was still married—technically. I was beginning to notice that in Italy, if you didn't go home to your wife, you also didn't file for divorce. A man could be married and live as though he were single, conducting a fully separate life, without social or moral consequences. The Italians seemed to accept the fact that when the fire between a couple had died out, it was all right to look for it elsewhere in another relationship. Recently divorced and disillusioned about marriage, Carla confided that her ex-husband had gone out every night, leaving her alone. She ruefully explained that he loved the night life, not the home life, and she'd been miserable married. She was again single, like me. Here tonight in this exquisite setting, Carla seemed comfortable with Primo. Primo not only had money, but he knew how to spend it, she later told me.

After we were seated in the center of a large dining room, all eyes and ears were fixed on me, it seemed. I was the newcomer, the only unfamiliar person at this exclusive members' club of Primo's. We were immediately served a glass of sparkling wine, prosecco, equivalent to having a first drink of champagne. Primo was in charge at all times, speaking about the club's golf, tennis and fine dining and planning the most delicious taste experiences for our table.

"Do you like prosciutto?" Primo asked me.

"I love it," I said.

"We will taste something locally raised and cured, like prosciutto but better. You will see," Primo said.

A platter arrived with thinly sliced *Bresaola*, garnished with black olives and thick shavings of parmesan cheese. My hosts explained that Bresaola was air dried and cured filet of beef, a specialty of the region. It was delicious.

"So, you are from New York? " Ambrogio asked, touching my forearm. I didn't find him good looking—maybe it was the weak chin—but he had a pleasant face and a full head of light brown hair extending off a deep forehead.

"Yes, that's where I lived until I moved to Rome in late November last year," I said.

"I go there often to visit my distributors. In Manhattan we work with Scalamandre," Primo said.

He may have seen my face go blank as he went on. "My business is textiles; we produce fine fabrics, such as jacquard, for quality interior designers. I travel all of Europe and the States representing the firm's fabrics. You probably have heard that Como is Italy's textile hub," Primo said.

"*Ho capito,*" (I understand) I managed to say between forkfuls of the bresaola. I had already had a second slice.

"You have a good appetite. I see that you like our food," Ambrogio said.

"It is delicious," I said. Primo looked pleased.

"*Va bene.* Would you like us to order the best dishes on the menu for all to taste?" Ambrogio said. "Or would you prefer to order yourself?"

"No, whatever you decide will be fine," probably conveying my consent as much with my face and hands as with my words. I tried hard to answer quickly and say what I wanted to say, but I heard a new accent in their rapid speech and it was a struggle. The three were very encouraging, and nodded in approval at whatever I said.

"In fact, I just returned from a visit to New York City in February," Primo said. "What a jewel of a city. There is no place else like it in the world. Only *che freddo* (what cold) we found in February."

I laughed, feeling more and more at ease with these two *simpatici* men who knew New York, traveled the world—hardly a provincial life-style—and were warm and encouraging. My doubts about fitting into the Italian culture—at least for the moment—were falling away, aided by the cordiality of my hosts and the effect of two glasses of sparkling wine. Ambrogio must have sensed my starting to relax.

"Ti vedo a tuo agio," (You look very much at home with us tonight) he said.

"It is the company," I replied. *Simpatica, molto simpatica.* Although it was hard to define, I understood what simpatico meant. Likeable and endearing. It was the right term for my new friends.

* * *

I would years later ask myself what Carla saw in me that reso-nated with her. We were both single and only about seven years apart in age. That's where the similarities ended. She came from a well to do background that allowed her to ski all season, stay in her own chalet in the mountains and belong to a golf and tennis club where she regularly played tournaments and won. She was an accomplished competitive athlete who never seemed obsessed with her prowess or her wins. She lived alone with her daughter, Silvia, now nine. She worked when her translating services were needed at the paper factories owned and operated by a pair of ancient uncles whom she described as *pesanti*, meaning they were querulous and tiresome. What struck me—at times moved me—was the sincerity and consistency of her commitment to our friendship.

I wondered if our roles had been reversed and I'd been introduced to a visiting Italian seeking to make a life in the States if I would have been as accepting, inclusive and nurturing. Could I have helped that person create a social life, meet new people, go out on the town, eat at fine restaurants and provide loyal companionship? The answer was that I probably wouldn't have, being the self-involved person I was at the time.

She had studied a couple of years at university and told me that when she met Luigi Spandri, the man she would marry, she lost interest in her studies. Luigi courted her in grand style. She confessed that because she was left without parents before she turned 20, his offer to get married and start a family had seduced her. The marriage didn't last, and she was convinced that she was far better off without a husband.

By the time I met her, she was enjoying Primo and his very grand lifestyle. Until she found out she was pregnant. Normally unflappable, Carla appeared upset with herself, self-accusing. Perhaps one careless night? I never knew. For several months we didn't see each other. When we did, she admitted having ended the relationship with Primo abruptly. She'd sought an abortion and told me it would have been unwise to try to do it in her home town of Erba. She'd made the 90-minute trip to Como City to avoid being found out, not just by her family and Primo's, but by her whole small town.

Despite my monogamous mindset, I couldn't help noticing that although men cheated on their wives all the time in Italy, it was done discreetly, with a genuine intent not to hurt their spouses, whom they rarely left, or their children. In some cases, when having a mistress was long term, wives tacitly accepted the situation as long as the family remained intact. Friends and family, even if not pleased, did not voice criticism. Were they embarrassed, given how common it was? Or since it wasn't spoken of, was it condoned? The Italians were wired to always present a good appearance, no matter what skeletons were rattled and rules were violated. Here was another instance of the tendency known as *fare bella figura*. The closest we non-Italians come to it is when we seek to "save face."

***

FRANCA AND VINCENZO

I probably took for granted how easily I was making new friends. Those who extended themselves and came to my rescue, as had Antonio and Salvatore; who like Franca and Vincenzo showered me with kindness and generosity and included me in the rituals with their family. Hanging out with them and their two children, aged eight and eleven, sharing a meal, listening to the banter between parents and kids, these were sacred rituals that I'd never even experienced in my own family. Growing up, my family was too fractured to enjoy pleasant conversation over dinner. On many occasions there was stone cold anger suppressed in silence, or full-blown arguments that ended in one or both parents raising their voices and storming off, hissing about loss of appetite. Is that a meager explanation for why being with my own family never made me feel at home?

I had met Franca through a mutual friend, Dario, who was an engineer working for L'ENIT, the national oil company. Sensing my desire for a lasting life in Italy and my openness to new friendships, Dario arranged for me to get to know Franca, a working woman whom he considered to be forward thinking. Then in Italy few women were raising children as well as working professionally full time. I invited Franca for a cappuccino and we took an immediate liking to one another. She was a petite, curvaceous woman, about 33, with glossy complexion, dark blonde, silky hair and a turned-up nose. She didn't look at all Italian to me, but more like a shorter version of the girls in the once popular Miss Rheingold (beer) beauty pageant, which took place in my home town every year. The contestants were beautiful girls with perfect complexions and gorgeous heads of fair hair. Franca was a wife, mother and an architect, who'd started working at age sixteen straight out of middle school, doing draft work in Vincenzo's architect studio. She started with no knowledge of architecture—all she could do was draw. Still, Vincenzo had taken her under his wing, and the two got married some four years later when she was 20. That's when she began her formal studies in architecture, earning a degree about seven years later while raising kids. This had occurred in the late '60s in Italy when it was rare for women from working class families to attend college and get a degree. Like me, Franca had left her home town to make something of herself, and she had chosen a career path that went against the mores of her own family and culture.

Whenever I called her, she would say: "Want to come for dinner at our house tonight? *C'è sempre posto per te.*" (There's always room for you.) That simple. And I grabbed at the invitation. She and Vincenzo, their kids, Lucca and Gabriella, and I sat down at a round table covered with a soft plastic, pastel tablecloth. Even after working a whole day and getting home at 6 p.m., Franca managed to fix dinner from scratch, the Italian way. Without fanfare, she'd prepare pasta, chicken cutlets Milanese, or maybe a beef paillard, thinly sliced beef sautéed quickly in oil and butter, vegetables, and sometimes a salad followed by fresh fruit for dessert and a slab of cheese. The platters would be passed around family style, and everyone shared. This made me feel more like one of them than a guest, and during the meal I could shed that "outsider" feeling.

"So, Lucca, how did your violin lesson go today?" Vincenzo asked.

"I started a new sonata," Lucca said. "It's by Scarlatti."

"*E molto bella,*" (It's very beautiful), he said.

I could see the rapture in his eyes even through his thick glasses. Lucca was 11. Vincenzo asked his daughter, Gabriella, who was just turning 9, about the new teacher in math class.

"To me, he's a prick," she said.

"That is not the way to talk about your teacher or anyone," Franca said emphatically. Gabriella made a face and looked at her brother, then sat up tall.

"*E vero*," (It's the truth) she said, not backing down.

"Vincenzo, say something to Gabriella," Franca said.

"Why do you think *cosi*?" (this way) the father asked calmly, holding his fork in midair, momentarily refraining from twirling spaghetti, and directing his gaze at his daughter.

"Well, because he couldn't solve one of the math problems, and I understood it right away, and I raised my hand but he wouldn't call on me," she said. "He told me I was interrupting the class. He is a prick and I hate him," Gabriella said.

Seeing his sister ready to cry, Lucca started laughing. Then she laughed, too. Franca looked very upset with her daughter and again asked Vincenzo to do something. Vincenzo was just finishing his spaghetti, scooping up the last of the sauce with bread. I really admired Vincenzo's restraint, so different from what I had seen at the dinner table growing up. In my family, people interrupted one another heatedly, often with disregard for whoever was speaking, and, at times they pounced, eager to point out blame.

"This is not the language you are allowed to speak," Franca said, continuing the dialog, which I translated as: "Gabriella, bella, don't you think you are exaggerating?" Franca said, more involved in the conversation than with eating, "This is my advice. Vincenzo, I want you to give yours. Gabriella, you are going to have to learn to be in class without irritating the teacher. Vincenzo, what do you say? *Cosa dici?*" Franca said.

Vincenzo held up the last piece of beef, looking for a taker. He placed it on Lucca's plate. Lucca was still not understanding his sister's dilemma.

"We are going to have to talk about this class," Vincenzo said finally. "Lucca, there is no reason to laugh. Gabriella, as we know, is very bright and the class may just be too slow for her."

"When you look like her, you can't be smart," Lucca said and got an elbow straight into his ribs from his sister. Lucca moaned and bristled.

"Well, at least I don't wear thick glasses that make me look like an old man," she fired back.

I had no experience with the dynamics of sibling infighting, which in later years I recognized might have toughened me, made me less defenseless in coping with life's small conflicts. I'd grown up as a late child, alone in the house with two quarreling parents, my older siblings already married or working and no longer living at home.

"*Vedi, Schiari,*" said Franca. (You see.) "This is what it's like to have two kids close in age and very intelligent, but not very respectful." She glared at her two children as she placed her two hands, fingers spread on the table, her elbows out to the side.

Then there was silence as everyone ate up what was still uneaten on their plates, dipping the soft inside of crusty bread in the juices from the sautéed beef and spinach. I had not spoken during most of the meal, not only for lack of a full vocabulary in Italian but also for lack of what to say as someone who wasn't a parent. The conversation at table triggered an awareness that my progress as a youngster at school had never been of interest to my mother and father: it was a non-topic. My parents didn't draw me out in a dialog. Their energy was consumed largely in carrying out the most basic responsibilities of parenting: putting food on the table, keeping a roof over our head.

And then there was tension between them that was thick enough to cut. Seeing Franca's eyes on me, I forced a smile in an effort to shake off these memories and revel in the harmony and love that permeated the Rainoldi family. They were a family who deep down took pride in one another's uniqueness, talents and accomplishments.

***

HIKING

Our day was entirely planned by Vincenzo, who was inclined to want a clear agenda and defined logistics. His professional title was Dottore Architetto Vincenzo Rainoldi, or Dr. Architect Vincenzo Rainoldi. Anyone who'd graduated with a baccalaureate in Italy earned the right to the designation of doctor. It was one common example of the Italian tendency toward overstatement. As an architect, Vincenzo was used to well executed plans, which may have contributed to his even-temperedness. I had observed that he was unflappable, including when he was around his feisty kids. Yes, I thought back in my room as I got dressed for the hike: he would be objective and take a neutral point of view. He is the perfect person to talk to about how to deal with Italian men.

We drove about a half mile to a parking area—call it base camp. We began by mounting a gentle slope, followed by a steeper one, and then the climb began. City girl that I am, I could boast walking for two miles on the streets of New York City and biking through Central Park as my most vigorous exercise to date. I didn't think attending jazz dance class at Carnegie Hall Studios with professional dancers counted. I excelled at freestyle dancing in smoky discos, but that didn't count toward being strong and fit either. I recognized that different muscles were being engaged in the act of hiking. In truth, I had led Franca and Vincenzo into thinking I was in better shape than I was. Knowing they not only hiked but skied, I had accepted their invitation without voicing my own doubts about being in shape. My stamina and muscle strength were likely to barely meet the challenges of the day's activities, compared to my friends, who were agile and muscular and demonstrated the ability to ply the rough terrain as they scaled the hillside. I had only two things going for me this morning: I was younger than my friends, and I wasn't a quitter.

"How much longer do we go straight up?" I asked, never imagining that coming down the hill would take more grip and grit. I could have stopped and turned around then and there, but I reminded myself that my hosts believed in my fitness, mistaking leanness for fitness.

"We are nearly half way to the first station, where we'll stop for lunch," Vincenzo said. "Then there's another loop if you want to go longer. *Tutto bene?*" (Is everything fine?) By then, I had taken up a distant third place, behind Franca, who was moving more slowly than I expected.

"I need you both to keep up with me, if you can. Am I going too fast?" Vincenzo asked, having kept a steady pace no matter what the incline.

Neither Franca nor I answered, putting every ounce of strength into keeping up and not falling way behind. I had worn boots, but they weren't for hiking; even with their corrugated sole, they weren't meant for hiking. To make matters worse, I wasn't able to take in my surroundings, barely lifting my head as I navigated the steep ascending path. A couple of times I tripped on some roots and realized that I had to place my foot firmly on the dried resin coated leaves or I would slip. Vincenzo came back to check on me and to keep me in the game. Without his thick glasses, he was quite handsome, his face smooth, his expression animated.

He said: "*Vai piano. Non c'e premura.*" (Go slowly. There's no rush.)

I welcomed that he was cutting me some slack. Maybe to cheer me, he remarked that it was an easy hike compared to what skiing involved. I quickly agreed with him, but secretly became alarmed, for I didn't know anything about the rigors of skiing either, and at that moment I regretted having ever embarked on the climb.

We arrived at a rest stop. Vincenzo took out his binoculars and panned the distant slopes. He showed me where a white dot or two equated to a private chalet someone had built into the mountainside. He was not out of breath, and only the beads of sweat on his wide forehead belied a modicum of exertion. Franca sat down and asked to borrow the binoculars. Vincenzo unloaded his backpack with our supplies, including food, and then he took off, saying: "*Torno presto.*" (I'll be back soon.) I think he felt we were holding him back, and I was glad for the time alone with Franca. She planted herself on a smooth rock and took a deep breath.

I plopped down, stretching out my legs, my calves tight as rubber bands. It was the hardest physical exercise I'd ever done. I wasn't sure I could get up and stand. To calm myself, I took out a cigarette and puffed on it, my lips almost too dry to hold the filter.

"So how did you do, *Schiari*," Franca said quietly. My friends often called me by my last name, my first name, Ruth, being unpronounceable in Italian.

Flicking the cigarette on a rock, I said: "Well, I made it up the mountain, that's all I can tell you. Climbing up is the hardest part, right?" My lungs were suddenly feeling the thinness of the air. My outstretched legs were quivering. We were both too drained of energy to care much about lunch: a sandwich and an orange for each of us plus a large bottle of water.

"What about you, Franca? You've done this many more times than I have." I noticed Franca get up very slowly and then sit down again, widening the fingers of both hands to comb her hair off her forehead.

Ciao L'Americana

"Was it a cinch?" I asked in English, waving my hand like a magic wand. She looked blank, not understanding.

"The hike—*era facile per te*, wasn't it easy for you?" I said with great emphasis on easy—*facile*. I could tell something was not quite right with Franca; she was pale, barely audible, and her normally shiny blonde bob was dull and matted. Pulling her knees up, she finally said: "I am a little weak today. The doctor told me to rest and take it easy for a while. But we had already made these plans to go hiking. Besides, Vincenzo loves to get away from Milan on the weekend."

I didn't know how deep I should probe into the mention of a doctor.

"I had no idea you'd gone to the doctor. When? Is it anything serious?" I asked.

"Just yesterday. He told me that he didn't think I should have another abortion; another would be too much for my body. I've already had 13," she said, her fingers on one hand stroking the inside palm of her other hand. She looked at me and I could sense a shadow cross her face.

It took some time for this to sink in. In the States, birth control pills were widely used by women who wanted to avoid pregnancy. I had used the pill. In Italy, I stopped taking the pill—too complicated to get a prescription. And Ray had used a condom and so did my first Italian boyfriend after him. At the age of 28, I had never been pregnant. I thought that abortions were what some single women had when they got pregnant by mistake and in my ignorance, I honestly didn't associate it with married women. As I pondered Franca's plight, I wanted to ask why she and Vincenzo had never used birth control. Couldn't Vincenzo put on a condom, for Christ's sake? Didn't he know what toll an abortion took on his wife's body? Or didn't she tell him when she went for the procedure? And even those who resisted birth control on religious grounds had a choice, as Catholic school had taught me many years ago. There was the rhythm method and, of course, abstinence. Franca and Vincenzo were free thinkers in a traditional society. They were left leaning and members of the Italian Communist party. They were in my mind an emancipated couple who both worked as professionals, raising a family without the help of a nanny or grandparents. It made me angry that my brave friend had been in the position of having to get an abortion, again and again.

But I said nothing. I looked down and picked up a twig, drawing lines in the dried earth, my throat gripping to think that Franca had used abortion as a means of birth control thirteen times.

"It may sound strange, Schiari," Franca said. "But it's been the right thing to do. I knew I only wanted these two children, the two are enough to raise."

I got up to give her a long teary hug.

"I understand, *ti capisco*. You've done the right thing. And you are a very good parent," I said, looking at Franca, whose moral compass had conditioned her choices. I was left with no argument.

"Now you see. After yesterday, I feel like a train wreck, Schiari," smiling with her mouth tight. She drank from the bottle of water. "I won't be able to do it again, according to the doctor—far too dangerous."

We heard a familiar voice calling from some distance away:

"*Arrivo*."

Franca rose and waved to Vincenzo, who had just come into view, blonde hair spiky and in disarray, his thick burgundy sweater filtering through the trees.

***

Ciao L'Americana

DOWNHILL

We had lunch sitting around a tiny crater in the ground which we covered with an old towel. It felt oddly like a resting place. Everyone had worked up an appetite by now and was ready to devour even the ordinary sandwiches we'd thrown together. Made of salami sweating with fat and flavor, soft cheese spilling over the edge of day-old bread, they were unexpectedly delicious. Vincenzo bit into an orange and peeled it with his fingers. He did the same for Franca and then he held up my orange, arching his eyebrows to ask if he should peel mine, too. I nodded. For mine, he fished out a military style pocket knife and peeled the orange in one continuous circle. I swallowed the last of my sandwich and ate the orange, which was a sweet, juicy finish to the salty taste of salami and cheese. I was too tired to help Franca and Vincenzo put everything in a trash bag and clean up. Barely able to get up from the ground, I wondered how I would summon the energy to go down the mountain.

"The descent is always easier, *non e vero*—right? What do you say, Vincenzo?" In a wild stab at humor, I called him "*il locomotore del giorno*," (the driver of the day). Those were the only words I knew that vaguely fit his unrelenting energy. He and Franca laughed at my trying to be funny in Italian.

"*Al contrario, Schiari* (On the contrary), it is a lot more demanding going down the slope because you have to grip with your thighs to balance the force of gravity that is already carrying you down," he said.

"It's like when a plane is landing and hits the runway at full speed. The pilot uses brakes, but also a counter brake system to resist the forward thrust and stabilize the plane. You hear it with every landing—the loud grinding noise."

Oh, God, I am in trouble, I thought. I only had my slim ballerina legs to stabilize me and they were already enormously sore.

Vincenzo was right, and I hated that he was right. Going down the hillside was much harder. I was on the brink of slipping and sliding most of the time and was forced to use extreme caution. I told my friends I would be moving slowly because I also wanted to see where I had been. The Italian Alps in that setting were an autumn haze. The trees were half empty of their brown and yellow gold leaves. The fallen leaves were poised on the surface of the slopes. At the edge of my sight line there was a funicular corridor, the red car faintly visible. On the lower slopes I was now tramping, pine and fir trees, their trunks astonishingly straight, had claimed their stakes. Every so often, pausing to look behind me as far as I could see, the depth of field brought into focus a thick forest that appeared to peak just below the clouds. I stopped every few minutes to move my head on its radius and try to lessen its weight on my shoulders. I had fallen way behind Franca and Vincenzo. From where I stood, the drop looked threatening; like a monkey, I began to use my hands to help me get down, fanny first. It was either slide on my butt or crawl in reverse because I couldn't grip the ground beneath me. My thighs were useless. My hands got chafed and scraped from contact with the rough surfaces. The descent had only made my body hurt more.

On the way home, I pondered how I would speak to Vincenzo. The kids were rowdy as they piled into the car and I screened them out, still trying to process what I now knew. Putting aside my indignity about Franca's abortions. I couldn't accept that he hadn't been complicit. But I suspected that Franca might have feigned fatigue or a migraine and not shown up to work in their architect studio to avoid explaining why she felt so depleted. *Just to prove that she was a loving wife.* Thinking about it, I concluded they just screwed like young rabbits, but at the expense of Franca's body. She was 33, but one day when she turned 40—with a body that had been subjected to stressful surgeries—she might appear 50. I felt sorry for Franca, yet I respected the fact that she had assumed responsibility for her pregnancies. Against all odds, Franca was really an emancipated woman.

We took a break and pulled into a distributor for gas and a soda. Vincenzo lifted the hood, muttering that he was afraid the motor was overheating. Franca took the kids off, trying to stifle their loudness. I waited for a moment when Vincenzo and I were alone.

"Vincenzo, you as an artist, a builder, a husband and father, what advice do you have for me about being with an Italian man? I would like to meet a man and have a serious relationship, not just an affair; you know, be taken in by his friends and meet the family—those kinds of things."

"Are you not finding Italian men who behave themselves with you?" he asked.

"It's not that they attack me or are brutes," I said, "just that I don't think they really can include me in their lives. I'm like a pet gazelle or a trophy date." My answer was not easy to express in the Italian I could speak, but he seemed to grasp its complexity.

"I see. That's a shame," he said. "It's unfortunate you have to suffer through that. But truthfully, I understand why," he said.

"You do?" I asked, thinking he was about to attack my character on some level to point out what I was doing wrong.

"Let me explain. This is a deep-rooted thing for men in Italy. It is said: *"Moglie e bue si prendono dal paese tuoi."* I understood that to mean: Wives and cattle come from your own country. "There is no changing that—it's ingrained," he said.

"So, Schiari, vedi—you see. No matter what you do or how you behave, you may always find that to be the case."

Should I believe this pronouncement? How retrograde, how primitive, I thought. It probably had not been easy for Vincenzo to share this about his own culture. I was relieved because at least it wasn't what I had done or how I'd behaved. Yet I was disappointed to hear that the way I was viewed was the problem: an American, not a native Italian; not living at home with parents, a visitor who wanted to stay, marry and start a family. Vincenzo was suggesting that the way Italians perceived me disqualified me as marriage material.

Franca returned from the toilet. She looked at me and said:

"What happened? You look upset. *Sconvolta*. Vincenzo, what's going on? What were the two of you discussing?"

"I'll tell you later," I said.

"No, tell me what's wrong," she insisted.

Vincenzo headed for the public bathroom and the kids were nowhere to be seen.

"Well, Franca, *ti spiego*. (let me explain) It seems every year right before my birthday, I feel a bit lonely, and I guess I start feeling sorry for myself."

"But why? Aren't you going to be celebrating your birthday and that you have your whole life ahead of you?" Franca wondered.

"It's not that easy to live here by myself. At times, I wish I had someone who could stick up for me, someone I could share the hard times with."

"That's certainly how I felt after leaving home at sixteen to go to Milan in search of work. I had nobody. My mother was completely opposed to my leaving. She screamed at me and told me never to come home again. But I wanted to get away from our small town. I could draw, and when I looked for work, Vincenzo gave me work. Later he gave me the chance to study."

"My mother, too, never has understood why I left home or what I am doing in Italy," I said.

"I understand how you feel," she was saying. "But you, you can do anything and you are free."

I began to tear up, turning away.

Touching my shoulder, Franca said: "You always have friends in us," and she hugged me.

For my birthday that year, Franca made me a Kelly green, wool pullover sweater with a delicate border of white and black diamonds across the collar bone. Franca had never taken a measure, yet it fit. I marveled at how many hours she must have spent knitting it. It was perfectly made. I didn't even know how to hold the knitting needles.

***

FILIPPO

My spirit was sagging under the weight of Vincenzo's revelation. By now, I was too far into creating my life in Italy to walk away. I was still hungry for new experiences, wanting and needing to fit in, and I continued to live with intensity. Yet I couldn't ignore my indignation that Italian men were seeing me through an invisible teleprompter that said: "She's American, single, liberated and loose." I clenched my teeth and inwardly cursed when I imagined how the women, too, may have imagined a teleprompter across my chest that said: "She's a foreigner looking for adventure with one of ours; she's a threat, a danger to us." If I had been inclined to accept those damning perceptions, I would have displayed my own message: "She's intelligent, well educated, passionate about living in Italy like a native. And vulnerable."

To be fair, when a man invited me to dine out, he didn't try anything sleezy on the first date. *I Milanesi*, whom I was meeting, had more class and savoir-faire than that. Besides, with few exceptions, neither Italian men nor women were "liberated." Men hadn't been exposed to the "my house or your house" proposition at the end of a date, which was emerging in the U.S. My Italian dates all behaved politely in the beginning. Now, are you ready for this reality? Most Italian men in their 30s and 40s—if single—wouldn't have been able to take me home to seduce me; they still lived with their mamas. These bachelors, known as *Mamisti*, took advantage of their privileges, courtesy of Mama: free rent, free laundry and housekeeping services and, of course, home cooked meals, courtesy of Mama. I was in safe territory until about the third date. There, in a nice restaurant, my date would focus on me over dessert and he'd begin to purr: "Oh, the city is so oppressive—it's been a rough week." *Tesoro, andiamo fuori citta.*" (Let's get away this weekend, darling.)

"Where to?" I would ask, always thrilled to get to know another corner of Italy, since every piece of it held a natural beauty for me.

"*In campagna.*" To the country villa.

I was so struck by the invitation that I didn't initially suspect any ulterior motive. I admit it took me a long time to figure things out, and by the time I did, I was disappointed and exploited by at least one or two lovers in the country villa. They were guys who expected—as though it were *de rigueur*—that I sleep with them.

By the time I met Filippo, I wasn't dating anyone, calling it quits, at least until someone came along who treated me with love. Empio, another architect friend, decided to introduce me to a buddy from university who was an architect as well. Empio assured me in his insistent southern Italian manner that I would like Filippo, and he made a point of saying that his friend needed to get out and start enjoying himself.

"Doesn't everyone? Please explain," I said.

He confided that Filippo had been married, but his wife had died tragically, leaving him with two little boys. "You've got to meet him," he effused.

"Okay," I said, my interest having been piqued at Empio's matchmaking. "I trust your judgment."

The two came to pick me up in Filippo's car and seated me in front. Already at the wheel, Filippo's physique was not discernable, but I observed his well sculpted head, healthy skin and chestnut hair that shone like the well-groomed hide of a prize stallion. His profile was classic Roman, his nose slightly curved. He exuded manly poise and presence. There was nothing awkward or boyish about him, and I wondered how much older than I he might be.

Empio had arranged for us to attend an event, a gala of some sort. When I walked into the banquet room with Filippo with his hand around my waist, I noticed people looking at us both, not simply staring at me, the foreigner. We made an attractive pair.

There was an orchestra warming up while people had a glass of wine. Empio brought us each wine, and it was so crowded around the drinks that we decided to sit down at a table. I could feel my face flushing with a new sensation swishing inside me; I felt a chemistry with his friend. It was useless to try to hide it. A few minutes later, Filippo rose and announced: "*Porto da mangiare.*" (I'll bring food.) Empio looked closely at me—he could read me—and smiled, pleased that he had been right. Filippo arrived with plates of food. The two college chums chatted easily and spoke rapidly. I strained to listen to them above the din of clanking plates, clinking forks and loud banter.

The band started up again and eventually switched to swing music—American lindy and jitterbug.

Filippo said: "*Ti piace ballare?*" (Do you like to dance?)

"I love to dance." I said. He led me to the dance floor as though our dancing was the most important event of his life. He moved gracefully for a tall, well-built man, had a keen sense of rhythm, and he could lead a turn precisely but gently.

"How is it you know how to do the jitterbug," I said, not concealing my surprise.

"*Mi e sempre piaciuto il jazz americano. Ti facccio vedere la mia collezione dei dischi.*" (I've always loved American jazz. I'll show you my record collection.)

"*Ho tutti i dischi di Nat King Cole.*" (I have all of Nat King Cole's recordings.) "Do you like him?"

"I love him," thinking this Filippo was a real find. He could dance swing and do lindy and jitterbug as if he'd done it his whole life. He knew my music.

"What about Frank Sinatra?" I asked.

"*Seenatra, certo. Come no?*" (Of course. He's the best; there's no one like him.)

He led me commandingly to our table and then went to get drinks. I followed him moving through the crowd, singling out his silhouette: black suit, white shirt, tie, polished shoes; his presence had weight. Gradually, we returned to the dance floor to the sound of slow music. He held me close, and I could feel the heat of his body as my cheek fit comfortably against his. We continued dancing, then to the jitterbug, until we were winded and sat down again. Empio had brought us dessert and was waiting for us to lift our forks together, a sort of toast. He looked at me and then at Filippo. If I were to read him, he would be thinking that his friend wasn't sad anymore. He was coming back to life with me and I would be good for him. I was already thinking that Filippo would be good for me. He shared my tastes and he appeared to love some things I loved, too: music, dancing, jazz, food. What more would I discover? I longed to become the woman who would stand beside him, a man completely at home in his surroundings, who could make me feel part of them.

I don't remember if we were so infatuated with each other that he brought me home that night or not, but if not, it was the next night. When it happened, I chuckled to myself that here at last was a man not living at home with Mama at age 39. I certainly remember the first time we made love. We were in his bedroom, lying on a puffy bed. At first I froze, feeling in my cells the ghost of his wife even as he seemed attentive and warm, kissing me with fervor. I coaxed him to lie down and be still, whispering: "*Ti prego, ho bisogno di un momento.*" (I need a moment, please.)

I got up and looked around, not turning on any more lights although the room was in semi darkness. On the bureau was an image of him with a woman, undoubtedly his wife who had died just fourteen months ago. I nearly gasped at how right for one another they appeared, for even their looks matched. Did I imagine a disapproving expression emanating from her photo? Or did her dead presence actually lead us to this bed to rekindle the Eros that I sensed so strongly between them in the photo. Was I the first lover for him since her death? I wondered if I was intruding. I couldn't control my mind nor my heart.

"How did she die?"

"It was a freak accident while we were away for the weekend with our little boys. She should never have been caught walking on that country road. I should have been the one who took the boys for a walk," his face growing rigid, his voice brooding.

"She was hit by a speeding car coming around a blind bend. The boys, who were behind her, ran to safety. She took the brunt of the impact and was killed instantly."

I got back into bed and snuggled into him, resting my chin on his shoulder. I wanted to hold him so tight it would squeeze out the still vivid memories. I didn't hear him cry and didn't see tears, but I felt his sorrow. I plied his silky torso with warm hands and a kiss or two. We didn't speak for a long time.

"Is this the same bed you shared?

He took time before answering.

"*Non c'e piu.*" (She's gone, no longer here.) He lay very still, as though he, too, were trying to process what was unfolding.

"*Tesoro, non ti preoccupare. Vedi come stiamo bene insieme.*" (Darling, don't worry. Look how beautiful we are together.)

Then he took me in his arms and pressed his broad chest against

Ciao L'Americana

mine, closing the space between us. He was tender, fiery and so much a man. In bed he convinced me that he was mine. Even with misgivings, how could I not have surrendered?

***

IN LOVE

To see his home in the daylight: a whole floor penthouse in a smaller building situated in the historic center of Milan, was to open my eyes to the chasm between the way I lived and his genteel standards. The furniture, some of it massive, was finely crafted of dark glossy wood; there were majestic mirrors, floors of marble or wood, Persian style rugs, several couches and a dining table for ten. Everything was of good taste and his home's appearance coincided with how I imagined a man like him to live. Filippo and I began to see each other every evening for dinner and I spent the nights at his place. There was no sight of his children. Although he didn't speak of his little boys, I sensed they were on his mind and I wondered why he was keeping them away from me. How sweet it would be to get to know two boys aged three and five who had lost their mother. I would have swooned. My intuition informed me that Filippo would shield them until he could present them with a proper mother.

About three weeks after we met, he had a party and introduced me to his closest friends. His friends eyed me with restrained curiosity, yet I could feel them looking me up and down. Were they pleased that Filippo was not drowning in grief, at least on the surface? As for heads that rolled at the sight of me in a mini dress with a deep scoop neck and lace-up bodice, in hindsight I wish I'd dressed more subtly. Slim and small breasted, I could pull off not wearing a bra, but in a purple mini dress, there was a lot of leg showing.

The social dynamics were predictably the same: nobody spoke English, and it was entirely my effort to express myself as gracefully as I could while fumbling to connect against all odds. Some of his friends were at least 20 years older than I. I did what came most easily. I showed appreciation for Filippo's sumptuous buffet, filling my plate with everything and eating with gusto. His friends expressed astonishment that a tall, skinny American girl could eat so much food. The cuisine had been prepared by his housekeeper under his careful direction, and it was clear that this kind of food evening in Filippo's household was not a first. Not all the dishes were known to me—even though I'd already lived and eaten in Italy for two and a half years. Hats off to him; today he'd be considered a "foodie." Nicely presented in beautiful ceramic and porcelain platters were marinated chicken breast, tortelloni with pesto, cheese focaccia, prosciutto with fresh figs, roasted peppers, shredded carrot salad with oil and balsamic dressing, bowls of grapes and for dessert, raisin ice cream, known as *gelato di uva*, similar to Häagen Das rum raisin, only better. The gelato was elegantly presented on a large silver platter in the form of balls, ready to be scooped up.

I was drawn to a man who enjoyed the best of life, beginning with fine food, wine and the home. Filippo, designer of buildings, both residences and public buildings and their interior spaces, was showing me the life he'd designed for himself. As he drew me into the scenario, I was falling in love with him.

We fed off that spark of sexual energy which had been there from the first moment. The connection between us gave me a feeling of belonging. And according to Empio, the connection between us was bringing Filippo back to life. If I could have put myself inside his skin, I was the lover capable of renewing him, and at the very least, distracting him. He had already revived his masculine drives, feeling lust, and the sex lifted his depression. As days and weeks went by, his restored manhood gathered momentum. He became playful for the first time, inventing a word for me: *Scimmia*, which means monkey. Even though I hated the term, I could tell he used it endearingly, and I backed off and let him tease me.

The other significant sign of his rebound was that he planned a three-week summer holiday for the two of us. It was downright romantic, and although I tried to take it nonchalantly, my fantasies about being with someone who could love me in style would not be quelled. I learned that he'd given the care of his two boys to his older sister, and he seemed at peace with the arrangement. Off we went by plane to the remote island of Sardegna to an isolated, self-contained resort. It was a bucolic environment meant for rest and relaxation for there was nothing to do or see nearby. We rose early, spent lots of time lying on the sand, staring through sunglasses at a deep blue summer sky and a calm aqua marine sea. As days went by, Filippo appeared untroubled, but not serene, adjusting to the new pace of doing nothing, while I was uncomfortable with the lack of conversation between us. It was simply too quiet. He virtually stopped talking, and I felt him retreating. He read, I read. We ate fabulous meals made with local Sardinian specialties—always the fish of the day. After lunch, we'd take a siesta out of necessity, knocked out by the effect of the high alcoholic content of Sardinian wine (15%) combined with the blazing midafternoon heat on the island.

He loved to cuddle in the water and play around, even have sex in the water, which was calm and clean. Even with the physical intimacy, I sensed a distance between us. With my often-alarming perceptivity, I sensed his holding back. I couldn't shake the feeling he was pulling away. Once while swimming, I asked about his children.

"You must miss them very much, no?"

"Of course. But they are in good hands with my sister. If it hadn't been for them, I don't think I would have made it. They are what I live for."

He'd never spoken that way and his candor was searing. Something in my gut drove me to find out more.

"What about loving someone again, the way you must have loved your wife?"

"Vedi, scimmia. The difference between the love you have for your children and the love for an adult, an equal, is like the difference between oil and water."

Regretting that I'd brought up the subject, my head was spinning with thoughts of being superfluous and unimportant, an awareness of not making the cut. We came out of the water in silence and walked toward the dry sand. I put on my sunglasses to mute the explosive red violet rays of the sun descending as we both sat on the towel and stared straight ahead. Some strange demon drove me to continue probing.

"So do you think you'll ever love again—deeply?"

I could feel him turn toward me, but was afraid to face him. I wanted to disappear yet needed to feel him close. I had gone too far; did I really want to know? Then I felt him get up and stand, taking in the mild sea breeze, intoxicating as it caressed us. From behind, I put my arms around him, gently rocking the soft, generous midsection of his body that I so loved. He must have known that I expected a response.

"*Per me, c'è solo un grand'amore nella vita.*" (For me, there is only one great love of a lifetime.) His tone was wise and wistful.

* * *

MALPENSA

I handed the bus driver my ticket to the airport and stood on the platform, my ankle boots rubbing against my luggage while I waited for him to load it on. Three supersized suitcases and my tattered nylon duffle were ready to go into the bowels of the Pullman. I stepped aside, waving my hand over the baggage.

"It's all mine," I said.

"*Prego*," he said, giving me a searching look as if he were aware there was a story behind all these bags.

"I am leaving Italy today," I said from behind large dark sunglasses.

I picked up my satchel, swollen with books and camera, which doubled as my purse, and then took off my sunglasses, my tired eyes sweeping the platform to make sure nothing was being left behind. I thanked the driver and handed him some Italian lire.

"*Prego*," the driver said, staring at the coins I'd put into his palm. He must have noticed the dark circles under my eyes. He gave me a tight smile and I glimpsed his yellow stained teeth and brown spotted hands.

"It's time for me to leave. It's time to go back."

"*Mi dispiace,*" (I'm sorry) he said. There was an awkward silence as he glanced around for other passengers. I was the last person to hand him a ticket.

"Is it time to board?" I asked, massaging my arms, which hurt from packing and handling my luggage. My stomach was woozy, too. For breakfast I'd had only a cappuccino, noting it was the last one I would have on Italian soil.

"Yes. It is now five minutes to seven and we will leave at seven, signorina," he said, his forefinger tapping his watch. I climbed onto the bus and took a window seat on the right in the third row with a direct view of the driver. Through a grimy glass window, I recognized the familiar gray of winter in Milan, where 49 degrees combined with high humidity and rolling fog felt as bone chilling as 29 degrees. The bus had no heat and to my relief, only a few passengers. Scattered mostly in the rear, these riders with squinting eyes, sealed expressions and slumped bodies seemed to be asleep. It was quiet.

I tightened the scarf around my head, fastened the top button of my coat and rolled up my collar. I suddenly felt exhausted, all my energy having been consumed by the departure. I'd had to clear out of a house I'd been sitting for a friend, leaving it immaculate, and then find a taxi to take me to the bus station before dawn to buy a ticket, all with luggage in tow. Sitting back in my seat, I let out a loud sigh. My neck felt as if it were on a string that was about to snap. My head held dead weight when I rolled it down and felt even heavier when I lifted it up. I angled it into the nook between the window and headrest, trying to get comfortable. I wriggled my cheeks, pretending the uphol-stery wasn't rough and ignoring how, in the raw dampness, it chafed my skin. Closing my eyes, I preferred to imagine the silky texture of Filippo's skin, the cheeks I loved to rub against mine. Touching them was enough to make the inside of my thighs throb. He could provoke a pulsating response by merely standing next to me in stillness, and he aroused a flurry of emotion which turned me into mush. I had always felt the magnetic pull between us. Whether or not it was pure animal attraction, and short lived, I was still in love with him. The depth of my feelings gave me a sense of belonging, of aliveness. On the rumbling bus, I thought about how we had been inseparable from the first night we met. Was such intensity destined to wane?

It is impossible to quiet my mind and sleep on the two-hour bus ride. I am powerless to stop my obsessing about the relationship and turning it over and over in my mind from the startling moment we returned from Sardinia. He saw me to my apartment and then left without a word of when we would see each other again. I felt as if he'd slapped me. Was it over just like that? The sting of rejection paralyzed me. For two weeks, I waited by the phone for his call—unable to bring myself to phone. I came up with a pretext and finally called, inventing a need to consult him about a design question. His voice was faint. He wasn't curt, nor was he warm as he doled out his professional advice. I told him how much I missed him. I refrained from saying that I can't sleep nights and have lost my appetite. Instinct told me I needed to be strong, show that I'm stable, not show my hurt. He sensed my desire to see him and made a date to get together later in the week. I was pleased, but still anxious.

After dinner, we went to my place instead of his. I learned he'd hired a governess for his two boys, who were again living full time with him. I threw my arms around him and stroked his face, trembling as I waited for him to kiss me. Instead, he said: "Why don't you do a little strip tease?"

"What," I said and laughed, puzzled and annoyed. He was subdued, not aroused. I decided to play the game, with no experience at all in waving scarves and prancing nude to excite a man.

"We should have some musica. Check out my records and choose something," I said.

The music will inspire me and get me going, I told myself. He fished through my vinyl collection and chose a recording of Italy's then favorite female crooner, Mina. The track he picked starts slow and then gathers momentum as her singing grows more intense, oozing raw emotion.

"So go on, go on. I dare you to find another woman who loves you more." Mina is wailing. The lyrics convey a kind of pathetic admission of love and devotion.

With all the bravado I could muster, I began to move, swinging a scarf in a spiral motion off my right hip. I tenuously removed my jewelry, my sweater next, and then velvet jeans until I got down to bra and panty, which I did not remove. Part of me wanted to shout: *"Basta! Enough with this charade."* I felt like throwing my hands up and asking **him** to undress me. He had always been irresistible: his dewy skin and firm body, proud head, cheeks like the inside of rose pedals, long legs entwined in mine.

The bus lurched and I opened my eyes, jolted out of my reverie. My fingers rubbed my nostril and I swear I could smell his clean scent of Pear's soap, a cruel trick of sense memory. The night I said goodbye I told him with a grave heart that I had decided to leave Italy. And he had told me after we made love that the problem wasn't with me, it was with him. He had lost all desire to carry on, even to sit down at his drawing table and work.

"Non ho motivo, mi manqua anche la voglia di lavorare. Non so cosa fare con me stesso in questi tempi." (I have no incentive. I lack the motivation to work. I don't know what I'm doing these days. I'm just muddling through.) Finally, he had opened up to me, admitting that he was in crisis. I pondered, with tears welling, what it meant for him to be so fractured. I held him tightly and he felt vulnerable, not fully present, as if he knew he was less a man and lover. While his behavior may not have had anything to do with me, as he insisted, how could I have helped him heal if he continued to withdraw.

My thoughts drifted to his confession on the beach in Sardinia about *il grande'amore*. I heard it as a romantic, yet fatalistic, concept. I had been plagued by what he hadn't said—about his wife, Lilly. Now almost a year later, I still had questions to ask even as I was leaving Italy and the relationship. I'd always wanted to know if he could ever escape feeling her presence in the home they'd shared. The girl in the photo on his bureau, her broad smile hinting at mischief, was she the great love of his life? These disabling thoughts haunted me. Would leaving Italy help me to leave them all behind?

Did Filippo start to withdraw from me because he couldn't get Lilly out of his cells? When we made love, was she the one he really embraced? Because I was so taken with him and he'd come on so strongly, I never thought he'd lose interest in me. At 29, I still had a lot to learn. It was Filippo who swore that in terms of the relationships that bind, he would put me into the category of water and his sons were like oil. Family were blood ties, impermeable and weighty. As he'd explained: "Water and oil don't mix."

If the bus driver had checked on his motley passengers, he'd have seen me raise my arms to reach for Filippo. He'd have observed me sniffling to keep from bawling, my hand clutching a tissue to blot away tears. I wasn't sure if I cried all the way to the airport because of a broken heart or because I was abandoning my dream of living forever in Italy. I rested my head on the seatback, willing these images to recede, sensing that I would never be the same. The airline terminals eventually came within view and the bus slowed and creaked to a stop.

Feeling less burdened, as if a dark cloud had lifted, I got off the bus lighter than when I had gotten on. With the driver's help I collected my bags and located a porter.

"*Si faccia coraggio, signorina,*" (Have courage), the driver said, as I thanked him and followed the porter into the Alitalia terminal to board the plane home to New York.

***

Ciao L'Americana

AFTERWORD

I left Italy, but it never left me. The much-loved persons, places, sounds and smells, compulsions and obsessions refused to fade. My eyes and ears remained attuned to Italy. Returning to New York after nearly four years, things happened that would not have happened had I not lived in Italy.

Aldo Gucci, head of Gucci Worldwide, the quintessential Italian leather maker, offered me a job. I had no retail sales experience; somehow I managed to impress him with my fluent Italian, distinct fashion style and confidence. He was notorious—I came to learn—for exploiting vendors by slashing their fees, overworking and underpaying employees, yet he hired me on the first interview at the salary amount requested. Although thrilled to work for a prestigious Italian company and report to the chairman, my enthusiasm was depleted by frequent episodes of his sexual harassment. I endured the job for just over a year.

A few months later, I was recruited to accompany a group to East Africa as assistant tour director of a travel series called Family of Man. Our group of sixteen educators thoughtfully witnessed how people lived throughout the countries we visited: Ethiopia, Kenya, Tanzania, Zimbabwe and Malawi. What a contrast to Italy where culture and the built environment celebrate centuries of art and architecture. Rural Africa exposed shelters made of dried mud or cow dung. Viewing Africans in their own land, often in conditions of extreme drought and severe poverty, observing children playing with mud instead of toys, observing animals in the wild while visiting the game parks, altered my sensibilities as a city girl groomed in the United States and Europe. My ambitions for exploring the planet became redefined. For the next decade I returned several times to Africa. Travel has since taken on a different sheen; I only visit the exotic and far flung destinations of the world, those that promise to be transformative.

If it can be said that any particular city felt like home, it would be New York. There I came to befriend the renowned chef Nanni, owner and executive chef of restaurants Nanni and Nanni al Valetto, both superb Manhattan eateries. My appreciation of *la cucina italiana* and the ease of communicating in his native language persuaded Nanni to share his methods of creating unfailingly delicious food. For more than a year, I immersed myself in his culinary treasures, taking notes and transcribing recipes for a cookbook.

Nothing shaped me more than my experiences in Italy: Ray's betrayal and flimsy character; the unfavorable beginning in Milan; Giuseppe's unwarranted generosity and remarkable grace; the stagnant and often evil minds of men in a patriarchal society; my own neediness and immaturity in relation to Filippo. All of it stretched me, the tears and anguish forming the texture of my life's tapestry.

Marriage was elusive to me in Italy, and it struck me that every foreign woman whom I saw in Italy was married to an Italian, as if that were her ticket into the culture, ensuring her acceptance. I wonder if being attached through marriage to an Italian would have given me a sense of belonging. Or would the reality of being an American have always hampered me, taking away my joy of fitting in. In reliving the experience in these pages, I have come to accept that I may never truly fit in anywhere; a sense of belonging is within or it's not.

***

Ciao L'Americana

The Rehearsal Club, 45-47 West 53rd, New York City, the original all female artist residence founded in 1913 where I lived briefly in the late 1960's as an aspiring actor.

Positano

Fontana di Trevi - Rome, Trevi Fountain

Colosseum - Rome

St. Peter's Basilica rises over the Tiber and Ponte Vittorio Emanuele II

Spaghetti with Mussels at Tonnarello in Trastevere - Rome

Inside Basilica Santa Maria Maggiore - Rome

The Roman Forum

Trevi Fountain, Rome's largest baroque foutain

Traditional whitewashed buildings - Puglia

Ciao L'Americana

Sanctuario dell'Addolorata - Molise, region (Abruzzo-Molise) where my parents were born

Rome eating, never a bad meal

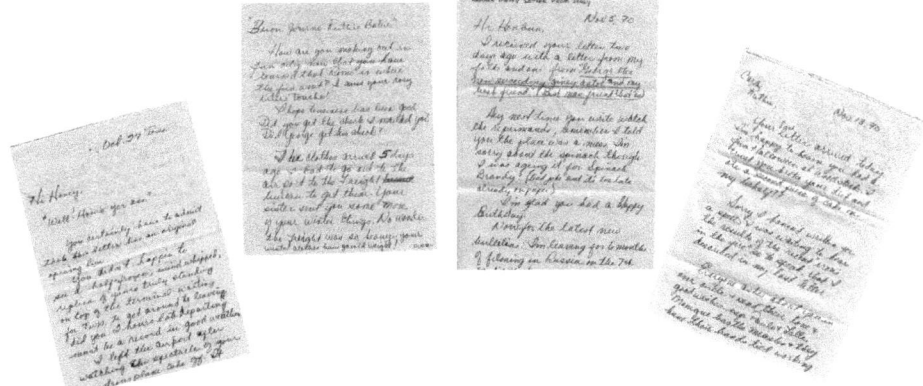

Ray's letters from Rome dated October 27 to November 13, 1970 prior to my rejoining him

With Ray

COLPO DI FULMINE DEL GIO

LIONELLO
CON UNA A

L'interprete di «Quinta stagione» è stato sorpreso per le vie di Milano teneramente abbracciato a Ruth Shari, l'attrice americana protagonista de «Il paladino». Fra i due non c'è solo simpatia ma si parla di folle amore e di... nozze

Si prepara una "Love story" in chiave italiana

L'amore dei giovani d'oggi come lo vede Ruth Shari che sarà l'interprete del film

GAETANO BASILICI

Dal 28 Gennaio al 3 Febbraio 1971

CINEMA 70 è una rubrica della domenica sera, come disse quel tale, fa più male al cinema che una battaglia perduta. E' una trasmissione fatta soltanto di parole in libertà riservata soltanto agli «addetti ai lavori». Noi a «Cinema 70» preferiamo «Ruth Shari 22»: è appena maggiorenne e vuol fare del cinema, quello vero naturalmente e non quello che ci gabella per tale la televisione. E per farlo, Ruth ha le carte in regola.

Coverage placed by journalist
Gaetano - Rome newspaper

Ruth Shari 129

Favorite Portrait

Fearless on the bike

www.ingramcontent.com/pod-product-compliance
Lightning Source LLC
Chambersburg PA
CBHW051630120626
46551CB00014B/2019